CULTURE MATTERS

THE PEACE CORPS CROSS-CULTURAL WORKBOOK

Peace Corps Information
Collection and Exchange
T0087

ISBN 0-9644472-3-1

ACKNOWLEDGEMENTS

The Peace Corps acknowledges the special efforts of the following people in the writing, editing, design, review, and production of *Culture Matters*: Raquel Aronhime, Laurette Bennhold-Samaan, Judy Benjamin, Brenda Bowman, Joe Byrnes, John Coyne, Amy DeWitt, Doug Gilzow, Rose Green, Lani Havens, Diego Hay, Steve Jacobs, Duane Karlen, Mary Jo Larson, Anne Latimer, Bill Perry, Jim Russell, Kathy Rulon, Craig Storti, and Patrick Triano.

CONTENTS ✀

INTRODUCTION 1

CHAPTER ONE—UNDERSTANDING CULTURE 5

1.1—Introducing Jan 6
1.2—Between the Lines 8
1.3—What Is Culture? 10
1.4—A Tough Moment 12
1.5—Linking Values to Behavior 13
1.6—Universal, Cultural or Personal 15
       Observation Activity 17
1.7—Universal, Cultural, or Personal—Making Observations 18
1.8—The Process of Cultural Conditioning 18
1.9—In the Mind of the Beholder 20
1.10—Defining Culture 25
Introducing Jan—An Analysis 26

FUNDAMENTALS OF CULTURE—INTRODUCTION 29

FUNDAMENTALS OF CULTURE I—
THE CONCEPT OF THE SELF 30

I.1—Sharing the Rewards 30
I.2—The Concept of Self—Individualism & Collectivism 31
I.3—Score Yourself—Individualist or Collectivist 34
I.4—Pleased to Meet You 36

CHAPTER TWO—
AMERICAN CULTURE AND AMERICAN DIVERSITY 37

2.1—Dear Todd 38
2.2—The Things We Say—Culture in Casual Expressions 41
       Informant Activity 43

2.3—Thirteen Cultural Categories—
  American and Host Country Views Compared
  Informant Activity 44
2.4—Thinking About My Job 51
2.5—Sources of American Culture 54
2.6—How Non-Americans See Americans 56
  Informant Activity 57
2.7—Learning About America 58
2.8—Now What? Diversity Critical Incidents 59
2.9—On Being Different 62
2.10—Parting Advice 63
Dear Todd—An Analysis 65

**FUNDAMENTALS OF CULTURE II—
PERSONAL VS. SOCIETAL OBLIGATIONS** **67**

II.1—An Accident 67
II.2—Personal and Societal Obligations—
  Universalism & Particularism 68
II.3—Score Yourself—
  Universalist or Particularist 71
II.4—Thinking it Through 73

CHAPTER THREE—STYLES OF COMMUNICATION **75**

3.1—Dear Gavin 76
3.2—Styles of Communication—Indirect and Direct 78
3.3—Clash of Styles? 80
3.4—Culture & Communication Styles—
  American and Host Country Views Compared 81
3.5—Nonverbal Communication—
  Gestures, Eye Contact & Conversational Style
  Observation Activity 84
3.6—Dialogues 88
3.7—Nonverbal Communication—
  Facial Expressions, Personal Space & Touching
  Observation Activity 91
3.8—Practicing Indirectness 96
3.9—Decoding Indirectness 97

3.10—Harmony and Saving Face 99
Dear Gavin—An Analysis 101

FUNDAMENTALS OF CULTURE III—
THE CONCEPT OF TIME 103

III.1—Service With a Smile 103
III.2—Concept of Time—
     Monochronic and Polychronic 104
III.3—Score Yourself—
     Monochronic & Polychronic 107
III.4—Indications 108

CHAPTER FOUR—CULTURE IN THE WORKPLACE 109

4.1—From Jan's Journal 110
4.2—Concept of Power—High & Low Power Distance 112
4.3—Trust 114
4.4—Dialogues 115
4.5—Attitude Toward Uncertainty & The Unknown—
     High & Low Uncertainty Avoidance 118
4.6—Dialogues 120
4.7—No Legs 122
4.8—The Source of Status—Achieved or Ascribed 123
4.9—Workplace Values and Norms—
     Comparing American and Host Country Views 127
4.10—Observing the Workplace
     Observation Activity 131
4.11—You Americans 134
4.12—Pacing 136
4.13—Turning the Tables 137
From Jan's Journal—An Analysis 140

FUNDAMENTALS OF CULTURE IV—
THE LOCUS OF CONTROL 143

IV.1—Who's In Charge Here? 143
IV.2—The Locus of Control—Internal & External 144

IV.3—Score Yourself—Internal and External Control 147

IV.4—Doing 148

CHAPTER FIVE—SOCIAL RELATIONSHIPS 149

5.1—Dear Jan 150

5.2—The Circle of Relations 152

    Informant Activity 154

5.3—Rules of the House—
    Interacting with a Host Country Family 156

5.4—The Limits of Friendship—
    What Do Friends Ask Friends To Do? 161

    Informant Activity 162

5.5—What Would You Do? 163

5.6—Family Life 166

5.7—Romantic Relationships 167

    Informant Activity 170

5.8—Men and Women—What Would You Do? 171

Dear Jan—An Analysis 175

FUNDAMENTALS OF CULTURE—COMPARING AMERICAN AND HOST COUNTRY VIEWS 179

CHAPTER SIX—ADJUSTING TO A NEW CULTURE 183

6.1—Dear Friends 184

6.2—Transitions 187

6.3—The Cycle of Adjustment 191

6.4—Settling In 196

6.5—The Little Things 198

6.6—The Four Levels of Cultural Awareness 199

6.7—Attitudes Toward Cultural Difference—
    From Ethnocentrism to Ethnorelativism 201

6.8—The Toughest Part 208

6.9—Coping Strategies 209

6.10—Can I Still Be Me? 213

APPENDIX—CONTINUING YOUR LEARNING 219

1—Using Cultural Informants 220

2—Joining In 222

3—Keeping a Journal 224

4—Learning From The Media and The Arts 226

5—Critical Incidents 229

6—Studying an Institution 230

ANSWERS 233

Chapter One 233

Fundamentals of Culture I 234

Chapter Two 235

Fundamentals of Culture II 238

Chapter Three 239

Fundamentals of Culture III 243

Chapter Four 244

Fundamentals of Culture IV 251

Chapter Five 252

Fundamentals of Culture—
        Comparing American and Host Country Views 253

Chapter Six 254

INTRODUCTION

Welcome to Peace Corps' cross-cultural training, one of the most challenging and rewarding dimensions of the toughest job you'll ever love.

This workbook, *Culture Matters,* is a map to guide you through your cross-cultural experience and also a way for you to record your thoughts and feelings as you live and work in your host country. It contains a variety of exercises, as well as stories and quotations from Volunteers who have served before you, from experts on cross-cultural training, and from the kind of people you might expect to meet in your new country. Their stories present the exhilaration, satisfaction, confusion, and frustration that are all part of being a Peace Corps Volunteer. These stories and quotations, we hope, will inspire you, sober you, make you laugh, and make you think. You can compare these sentiments to your own observations and reactions as you move deeper into the culture around you.

We all would like to find a magic pill for crossing cultures, the "right" answer, a simple list of do's and don'ts, and you will get some useful do's and don'ts from your trainers. But crossing cultures is a dynamic, complex process, where context is everything. A list of behaviors or a script can only take you so far, for what is a "do" in one set of circumstances might very well be a "don't" in another. This workbook will help you function outside the script, to understand the values and beliefs behind behavior, and, ultimately, how the local people think.

Cross-cultural training involves not only learning about the place you've come to, but comparing it to what you've come from-to the assumptions and values that have shaped you. In *Culture Matters,* therefore, you will be examining the behaviors and values of people in your host country in relation to those of people in your own. This workbook does not intend to suggest that American culture is necessarily superior or inferior to your host country's culture.

MAKING SENSE OF YOUR EXPERIENCE

You may wonder why you need such a workbook since you are, after all, living in the country and may even be living with a host family. Living in the country does expose you to the host culture, of course, but cross-cultural exposure is not cross-cultural knowledge. Having an experience, in other words, does not necessarily mean understanding it. You need to make sense of the contact you're having, which is what cross-cultural training and this workbook are designed to do.

Mystery is delightful and exciting, but it is foolish to admire it too highly. A thing is mysterious merely because it is unknown. There will always be mysteries because there will always be unknown and unknowable things. But it is best to know what is knowable.

—*Aldous Huxley,*
<u>*Along the Road*</u>

You may understand much of what's been happening to you, but many actions, attitudes, values—entire ways of thinking and behaving—may on occasion surprise, puzzle, or even shock you. On the other hand, you also may be unaware of what you have in common with host country nationals. People in any culture, for example, need to find an acceptable way to express anger, cope with sadness, manage conflict, show respect, demonstrate love, or deal with sexuality. As we examine the differences between two cultures, we are often looking at different ways of answering the same questions. If you don't notice the similarities, it's because the ways in which we act or think differently are what produce the most challenge and tension for us. What we have in *common* often goes unnoticed, but it is one of the most important parts of the Peace Corps experience.

THE GOAL IS UNDERSTANDING

In cross-cultural training and living, the goal is learning about yourself and others. Just as you want to learn another language so that you can communicate with local people and understand the new world around you, you also will want to learn the silent language of cultures—your own and your host country's.

In trying to appreciate the differences between your culture and the local one, you may feel that you're supposed to like and accept all these differences. Cultural sensitivity, however, means knowing about and respecting the norms of the local culture, not necessarily liking them. You may, in fact, be frustrated or even offended by certain acts. In some cases, increased understanding will lead to greater respect, tolerance, and acceptance; in others, it just leads to enhanced awareness. The goal in cross-cultural training is to increase your understanding, to give you a powerful set of skills, a framework to make sense of whatever you do and experience as a Volunteer so that you will be able to interact successfully with host country people. That is what will make you an effective Peace Corps Volunteer.

A COUPLE OF CAVEATS

It's impossible to talk about groups of people without generalizing, but without talking about groups, we can't talk about culture. In order to contrast and compare US Americans* and host country people, this workbook asks you to make a number of generalizations. Treat these generalizations with skepticism and wariness. They can give you potentially accurate and useful information, but the actual accuracy and usefulness will depend on the context and specific circumstances.

* For brevity and simplicity, we will use the term Americans to refer to US Americans. We do, however, wish to acknowledge a global perspective by recognizing those outside our nation's borders who share in the heritage of the name "America."

Americans, for example, may be regarded as individualists, but in some circumstances, Americans will be highly team oriented. Another concern with generalizations is that we instinctively feel uncomfortable making them or being the subject of them. They rob us of what makes us unique. To allow you to express your individuality, this workbook wherever possible gives you an opportunity to consider and record your personal views.

Keep in mind, too, that culture is just one of numerous influences on behavior. People can differ from each other in many other aspects as well. Could the miscommunication or misunderstanding between you and a host country national be the result of a difference in personality, age, generation, or gender, and not a cultural difference? Maybe you misinterpreted her or she misinterpreted you because she grew up in a city and you grew up on a farm. As you try to understand the role culture plays in behavior, remember that personal differences often play as great or even a greater role.

USING THIS WORKBOOK

Culture Matters has been designed mainly for independent study. You should move through the workbook at your own pace. On occasion, your trainers may conduct group sessions that deal with the same concepts covered in these pages, giving you the chance to share some of your feelings and reactions with other trainees and to hear theirs. In doing a number of the activities in this workbook, you will be asking questions of your host country friends, who will act as your cultural informants. Be ready for conflicting replies; that's part of the richness of culture.

Use the workbook in the ways that suit you. Some of you may complete every exercise your first few weeks in country; others of you may work with certain chapters in training, and other chapters after you have become a Volunteer, when the content of those sections suddenly has meaning or relevance for you. You may never want to do certain activities while you may want to do others repeatedly, at different times during your service. You may even want to refer to this workbook when you share your cross-cultural experiences back home. Revisit sections over time, browse, analyze, question, ponder, and enjoy.

However you approach this workbook, you will always have it as a record of your personal journey into the host culture, a journey that is one of the greatest legacies of the Peace Corps experience.

CHAPTER ONE ✦ UNDERSTANDING CULTURE

This workbook begins by defining a few terms and inviting you to consider some of the key processes and concepts embodied in this word, "culture." Before you look at any culture in particular, it is helpful to understand what culture in general is and how it works.

The central focus here is on the relationship between culture in the abstract—the underlying values and assumptions of a society—and culture in the flesh—the specific behaviors that derive from those values. It is important to understand that what people do and say in a particular culture, whether it be yours or that of your host country, are not arbitrary and spontaneous, but are consistent with what people in that culture value and believe in. By knowing people's values and beliefs, you can come to expect and predict their behavior. Once host country people are no longer catching you off guard with their actions and once you are no longer simply reacting to their actions, you are well on your way to successful cultural adjustment.

Moreover, once you accept that people behave the way they do for a reason, whatever you may think of that reason, you can go beyond simply reacting to that behavior and figure out how to work with it. Knowing where host country behavior is coming from doesn't mean that you have to like or accept it, but it should mean that you're no longer surprised by it—and that is a considerable step toward successful interaction.

Finally, in this chapter, you discover what this workbook is *not* going to be about—that is, the universal behaviors that are common to all cultures and the personal behaviors that are specific to every individual. These are important topics, but they are beyond the scope of this book— except to remind you that because of universal behaviors, you may not be surprised nor confused by many of the ways host country people act, while because of individual differences, you may not expect nor understand what someone says or does even after you've learned about the host country culture in general.

> *What I say is this, and this I do not say to all Englishmen. God made us different, you and I, and your fathers and my fathers. For one thing, we have not the same notions of honesty and speaking the truth. That is not our fault, because we are made so. And look now what you do? You come and judge us by your own standards of morality. You are, of course, too hard on us. And again I tell you you are great fools in this matter. Who are we to have your morals, or you to have ours?*
>
> —*Rudyard Kipling,* <u>*East and West*</u>

Note— Trainees who are living with host families may want to read and complete Exercise 5.3, p. 156, "The Rules of the House," in Chapter Five, before continuing further in this workbook. This exercise has information useful at this stage of your experience.

1.1—INTRODUCING JAN ᔕ

In this workbook, you meet a fictitious Peace Corps Volunteer (PCV) named Jan, whom you follow via letters and extracts from her journal through the various phases of her Peace Corps experience, from pre-service training to the end of her service. You catch up with Jan at the beginning of each chapter, where you get an update on what's happening in her life.

In each of these excerpts, including the one that follows, Jan makes some observations or reaches some conclusions about the experience of living and working overseas that may not be altogether complete or accurate, however real and heartfelt they may be to her. These observations or comments are keyed to the information covered in that particular chapter, and your task in each case is to read this latest communication from Jan and mark any passages that seem suspect or dubious to you. After you work through the various activities in the chapter, you are asked to look at Jan's remarks again, in light of what you have now learned, and see if you would mark the same passages or add any others. The paragraphs are numbered for ease of reference.

Sunday, June 27

1. *It has been so hectic in the 10 days we've been here. I've only had time to make notes for this journal. Now, at last, I can write a real entry. It's Sunday afternoon and for once we have nothing official scheduled. My clothes are drying on the line (I have to sit here and watch them, my host mother told me, because "bad people" may come and steal them) and I'm sitting in the shade of some kind of fruit tree.*

2. *I'm not so sure about those bad people, for I've certainly not met anyone yet who fits that description. Everyone we've met so far, from the training staff to our host families, has been remarkably kind and nice. It's a cliche, I know, but the people really are exceptionally nice; they can't do enough for you, and, much to my surprise, they understand us much better than I thought they would.*

3. *Maybe understand isn't the word. Maybe the real point is that they just aren't as different as I thought they would be or was led to believe they would be. Or maybe it's that in spite of a few superficial differences, in clothes, food, dress, that underneath they are more like us than I thought. Why do I say this? It's just that there haven't been any real disasters yet; I haven't done anything that has shocked or offended anyone. I suppose it's because I learned a lot of the do's and don'ts from that culture-shock book I read before coming here that I can get by without making any major mistakes. And I certainly haven't observed anything that really shocked or offended me.*

4. *I really do understand more than I expected to (not the language, of course, but the things people do) and recognize a lot of common behaviors. I watched people in a restaurant the other night, and there was nothing they did that I wouldn't do back home. On the other hand, come to think of it, I did see someone kick a dog the other afternoon and was shocked at such casual cruelty.*

5. *I have a lot to learn, I'm sure, but if these first few days are any indication, this is not going to be quite as hard as I had expected.*

1.2—BETWEEN THE LINES ℘

To begin thinking about culture, read carefully the following statement that describes a classroom in a developing country as seen by an American observer.*

> *Teachers' frequent use of corporal punishment discourages students from actively participating in the classroom. Students are expected to sit rigidly in their seats and speak only when spoken to. Conditioned in this way, it's not surprising they don't feel free to speak out in the classroom; their shyness, however, should not be mistaken for lack of interest.*

If you read between the lines, you see that the writer makes a number of assumptions about children, students, teachers, and the way people learn. Before reading further, list as many of these beliefs or assumptions as you can in the space below.

1. *that student participation in class is good.*

Culture is the shared set of assumptions, values, and beliefs of a group of people by which they organize their common life.

—Gary Wederspahn

2. _____

_____

3. _____

_____

4. _____

_____

5. _____

_____

6. _____

_____

The source for this exercise is Dr. Robert Kohls.

You could have found some or all of the following beliefs:

1. that student participation in class is good.
2. that corporal punishment of young people is bad.
3. that sitting rigidly is bad for young people.
4. that speaking only when spoken to is bad.
5. that speaking freely is good.
6. that students who don't speak are shy.
7. that lack of interest is bad.

—INSIGHT—
When we look at behavior, we interpret what is happening through the filter of what our culture *tells* us is happening.

Now imagine for a moment a culture in which people do not share these beliefs, whose people, in fact, believe the opposite. How would they view the same classroom? How would they view a classroom in the United States? That people from two different cultures can view the same behavior differently is precisely what makes cross-cultural encounters so challenging and problematic.

1.3—WHAT IS CULTURE? ✍

THE ICEBERG

Culture has been aptly compared to an iceberg. Just as an iceberg has a visible section above the waterline, and a larger, invisible section below the water line, so culture has some aspects that are observable and others that can only be suspected, imagined, or intuited. Also like an iceberg, that part of culture that is visible (observable behavior) is only a small part of a much bigger whole.

The numbered items that appear below are all features of culture. In the drawing of the iceberg on the opposite page, write above the waterline the numbers for those features you consider observable behavior; write the remaining numbers beneath the line.

1. facial expressions
2. religious beliefs
3. religious rituals
4. importance of time
5. paintings
6. values
7. literature
8. childraising beliefs
9. concept of leadership
10. gestures
11. holiday customs
12. concept of fairness
13. nature of friendship

14. notions of modesty
15. foods
16. eating habits
17. understanding of the natural world
18. concept of self
19. work ethic
20. concept of beauty
21. music
22. styles of dress
23. general world view
24. concept of personal space
25. rules of social etiquette

—INSIGHT—

Surface behaviors are influenced by beneath-the-surface values and assumptions.

You can see that there is a relationship between those items that appear above the waterline and those that appear below it. In most cases, the invisible aspects of culture influence or cause the visible ones. Religious beliefs, for example, are clearly manifest in certain holiday customs, and notions of modesty affect styles of dress.

[Suggested answers to the exercise appear on page 233.]

1.4—A TOUGH MOMENT ෨

Think of the worst experience you've had in country so far— either a moment when you've been most frustrated, embarrassed, confused, or annoyed, or something that bothers you on a daily basis. What in your cultural background made you react so strongly? Is there a cultural explanation? Do you think local people would have reacted the same way? Why, or why not?

Culture consists in patterned ways of thinking, feeling and reacting. The essential core of culture consists of traditional ideas and especially their attached values.

—Clyde Kluckhohn

1.5—LINKING VALUES TO BEHAVIOR ᔫ

In the iceberg exercise, you saw how certain aspects or features of culture are visible— they show up in people's behavior—while many other aspects of culture are invisible, existing only in the realms of thought, feeling, and belief. The examples in this exercise show how these two realms, the visible and the hidden, are related to each other, how the values and beliefs you cannot see affect behavior.

To understand where behavior comes from—to understand *why* people behave the way they do—means learning about values and beliefs. The behavior of people from another culture may seem strange to you, but it probably makes sense to them, and vice versa. The reason *any* behavior makes sense is simply because it is consistent with what a given person believes in or holds dear. Conversely, when we say that what someone has done "makes no sense," what we mean is that that action contradicts what we believe that person feels or wants.

In the exercise below, match the value or belief in the column on the left to a behavior in the column on the right.

1. Directness	_____ Use of understatement.
2. Centrality of family	_____ Asking people to call you by your first name.
3. External control	_____ Taking off from work to attend the funeral of an aunt.
4. Saving face	_____ Not helping the person next to you on an exam.
5. Respect for age	_____ Disagreeing openly with someone at a meeting.
6. Informality	_____ Not laying off an older worker whose performance is weak.
7. Deference to authority	_____ At a meeting, agreeing with a suggestion you think is wrong.
8. Indirectness	_____ Inviting the teaboy to eat lunch with you in your office.
9. Self-reliance	_____ Asking the headmaster's opinion of something you're the expert on.
10. Egalitarianism	_____ Accepting, without question, that something cannot be changed.

[For suggested answers, see page 233.]

> *Culture consists of concepts, values, and assumptions about life that guide behavior and are widely shared by people....[These] are transmitted generation to generation, rarely with explicit instructions, by parents...and other respected elders.*
>
> —*Richard Brislin & Tomoko Yoshida*

—INSIGHT—

Behavior makes more sense when you understand the value or belief behind it.

BATTERIES

I hadn't timed it right. The village I had to get to was still an hour away when night fell. Walking in the dark was a nuisance; also, it had been raining since early afternoon. Worst of all, as I leaned against the wall of the chautara and felt the blessed release from the weight of my backpack, I discovered my flashlight batteries were dead. The hour ahead was shaping up poorly.

As I stood there in the rain, my glasses fogged, drinking from my water bottle, an old woman came around the bend, bent over under a stack of firewood. She headed for the chautara, her eyes down, and nearly walked into me, looking up suddenly when

she saw my feet. "Namaste," she said, shifting her load onto the wall. "Kaha jaane?"

"To the village," I said.

"Tonight? It's dark and your shirt is wet." Then, more urgently, "You're the American, aren't you?"

"My son is in America," she said. She didn't look like the type whose son would be in America. "He joined the army, the Gurkhas, and they sent him there for training. Three months ago. He's a country boy. I worry. You need some tea before you go on."

After ten minutes, we were at her small house beside the trail. She doffed the firewood and turned to me, "Take off your shirt." I looked surprised. "I'll dry it by the fire in the kitchen. Put on this blanket."

A few minutes later she came out of the kitchen with two mugs of tea, swept a hapless chicken off the table, and pulled up a bench for me. The tea worked wonders, bringing back my courage for the walk ahead. She offered me food, too, but I declined, explaining that I didn't want to be on the trail too late at night. "It's OK," she said. "You have a flashlight."

She fetched my shirt. I put it on, revived by the warmth against my skin, and went outside to hoist my pack. I turned to thank her. "Switch on your flashlight," she told me.

"The batteries are dead." She went inside and came back with two batteries, a considerable gift for someone of her means.

"I couldn't," I said. "Besides, I know the trail."

"Take them." She smiled, showing great gaps where teeth had once been.

"You've been very kind to me," I said.

"My son is in America," she said. "Some day, on the trail, he will be cold and wet. Maybe a mother in your land will help him."

—PCV Nepal

1.6—UNIVERSAL, CULTURAL OR PERSONAL ✍

Culture is only one category or dimension of human behavior, and it is therefore important to see it in relation to the other two dimensions: the universal and the personal. The three can be distinguished as follows:

- ✪ *universal* refers to ways in which all people in all groups are the same

- ✪ *cultural* refers to what a particular *group* of people have in common with each other and how they are different from every *other* group

- ✪ *personal* describes the ways in which each one of us is different from everyone else, including those in our group

These are two important points for you to remember:

1. Because of universal behavior, not everything about people in a new culture is going to be different; some of what you already know about human behavior is going to apply in your host country.

2. Because of personal behavior, not everything you learn about your host culture is going to apply in equal measure, or at all, to every *individual* in that culture.

Culture is the outward expression of a unifying and consistent vision brought by a particular community to its confrontation with such core issues as the origins of the cosmos, the harsh unpredictability of the natural environment, the nature of society, and humankind's place in the order of things.

—Edward Hall

This next exercise contains a list of behaviors. In the underlined space preceding each of them, put a "U" if you think the behavior is universal, "C" if it is cultural, or "P" if it is personal.

1. _____ Sleeping with a bedroom window open.

2. _____ Running from a dangerous animal.

3. _____ Considering snakes to be "evil."

4. _____ Men opening doors for women.

5. _____ Respecting older people.

6. _____ Liking spicy food.

7. _____ Preferring playing soccer to reading a book.

8. _____ Eating regularly.

9. _____ Eating with knife, fork, and spoon.

10. _____ Being wary of strangers.

11. _____ Calling a waiter with a hissing sound.

12. _____ Regretting being the cause of an accident.

13. _____ Feeling sad at the death of your mother.

14. _____ Wearing white mourning robes for 30 days after the death of your mother.

15. _____ Not liking wearing mourning robes for 30 days after the death of your mother.

[For suggested answers, see page 233.)

—INSIGHT—

Some behaviors are shared by us all, while some others are unique to individuals.

1.7—UNIVERSAL, CULTURAL, OR PERSONAL—MAKING OBSERVATIONS ✍

The differences between universal, cultural, and personal behaviors occur in all cultures. Try to find examples of each in your host country. Spend some time in the streets observing the people around you and try to note four examples of each category of behavior. For personal behaviors, you may find it easier observing people you know well, such as people at your training site or in your host family. When you have completed this exercise, it may be helpful to show your list to someone else to get that person's reactions.

UNIVERSAL

1. _____

2. _____

3. _____

CULTURAL

1. _____

2. _____

3. _____

PERSONAL

1. _____

2. _____

3. _____

1.8—THE PROCESS OF CULTURAL CONDITIONING 🐾

Culture is an integrated system of learned behavior patterns that are characteristic of the members of any given society. Culture refers to the total way of life for a particular group of people. It includes [what] a group of people thinks, says, does and makes—its customs, language, material artifacts and shared systems of attitudes and feelings.

—Robert Kohls

How do people *acquire* their culture? How do they learn all the behaviors that are regarded as right and wrong in their society? This process, known as cultural conditioning, goes on in all cultures, but the specific behaviors that people acquire, the precise content of their conditioning, varies considerably from group to group. Keep in mind also that while it is behaviors that people learn through this process, they are automatically learning and internalizing the values and beliefs behind those behaviors. When you understand how this process works, you can then understand how two people from different cultures can behave in radically different ways and both be completely convinced they are right.

While conditioning occurs mostly in early childhood, adults continue to be conditioned as they acquire new behaviors throughout their life. The differences between the two are these:

1. In **Childhood** conditioning, infants and young children learn such basic activities of life as eating, walking, talking, dressing, bathing, etc.

2. In **Adult** conditioning, people learn new behaviors or new ways to perform already conditioned behaviors, as, for example, learning to use a Turkish toilet or eat with your hands rather than with silverware.

Though the steps are the same in each case, one difference in adult conditioning, the kind most PCVs experience, is that it often requires *un*learning or *un*acquiring behavior that was already acquired through childhood conditioning, and this can take longer. Here are the five steps in the process of cultural conditioning.

1. **Observation/Instruction**—At this stage, you are only beginning to become aware of a particular behavior but have not yet tried to do it yourself. Taking the example of eating with your hands, you may have observed how it is done, or someone may have told you how it is done.

2. **Imitation**—Now you actually try to carry out the activity; you sit down at a table and begin eating with your hands. At this stage, it is awkward for you, and you're conscious all the while of what you're doing, trying not to make mistakes. You may have difficulty concentrating on a conversation, for all your attention is on the act of eating.

3. **Reinforcement**—As you eat, people encourage you when you do it right and correct you when you are wrong. Over the course of several meals, you naturally try to do what they tell you.

4. **Internalization**—Without needing much reinforcement, over time and with practice, you now know how to eat with your hands. You may still have to pay attention to what you're doing, but not as much as during stages 2 and 3.

5. **Spontaneous Manifestation**—Now you're able to eat "the right way" without paying any conscious attention to what you're doing. It comes naturally; as you eat, you're aware of other things, not the act of eating.

Now try to think of various behaviors you are in the process of learning or relearning as you adjust to your host country and what stage you are in vis-a-vis that behavior. Try to write down a behavior for each of the five stages as you think of the following:

—INSIGHT—

While people have to learn most of their behavior, after they learn it they come to regard that behavior as natural and normal— for everyone.

1. Something you are just becoming aware of and perhaps observing closely but not yet doing.

   _____

2. Something you have just begun to try doing.

   _____

3. Something you've done once or twice but haven't mastered yet.

   _____

4. Something you have recently mastered.

   _____

5. Something you now do without thinking.

   _____

1.9—In the Mind of the Beholder ✍

We all believe that we observe reality, things as they are, but what actually happens is that the mind interprets what the eyes see and gives it meaning; it is only at this point, when meaning is assigned, that we can truly say we have *seen* something. In other words, what we see is as much in the mind as it is in reality. If you consider that the mind of a person from one culture is going to be different in many ways from the mind of a person from another culture, then you have the explanation for that most fundamental of all cross-cultural problems: the fact that two people look upon the same reality, the same example of behavior, and see two entirely different things.

Any behavior observed across the cultural divide, therefore, has to be interpreted in two ways:

❥ the meaning given to it by the person who *does* the action, and

❥ the meaning given to it by the person who *observes* the action

Only when these two meanings are the same do we have successful communication, successful in the sense that the meaning that was intended by the doer is the one that was understood by the observer.

Part One

In the first part of this exercise, read the description of the eight instances of behavior given below and write down your immediate response to or interpretation of that behavior in terms of your own cultural values, beliefs, or perception. The first one has been done for you.

1. A person comes to a meeting half an hour after the stated starting time.

    Your interpretation: *This person is late and should at least apologize or give an explanation.*

2. Someone kicks a dog.

    Your interpretation: _____

    _____

3. At the end of a meal, people belch audibly.

   Your interpretation: _____

   _____

4. Someone makes the OK gesture at you.

   Your interpretation: _____

   _____

5. A woman carries a heavy pile of wood on her back while her husband walks in front of her carrying nothing.

   Your interpretation: _____

   _____

6. A male guest helps a hostess carry dirty dishes into the kitchen.

   Your interpretation: _____

   _____

7. A young man and a young woman are kissing each other while seated on a park bench.

   Your interpretation: _____

   _____

8. While taking an exam, a student copies from the paper of another student.

   Your interpretation: _____

   _____

PART TWO

In the second part of this activity, you are asked to imagine how these same eight behaviors would be perceived or interpreted by someone from a culture different than your own. The particular cultural difference is described in each case. Read each behavior and the description of the culture, and then write in the space provided how you think a person from such a culture would interpret that behavior.

1. A person comes to a meeting half an hour after the stated starting time. How would this act be interpreted:

   ❂ *by someone from a culture where people always arrive half an hour after the stated starting time*

   Interpretation: _____

   _____

   ❂ *by someone from a culture where meetings never start until at least an hour after the stated time*

   Interpretation: _____

   _____

2. Someone kicks a dog. How would this act be interpreted:

   ❂ *by someone from a country where dogs always carry disease*

   Interpretation: _____

   _____

   ❂ *by someone from a country where most dogs are wild and vicious*

   Interpretation: _____

   _____

3. At the end of a meal, people belch audibly. How would this be interpreted:

   ❂ *by someone from a culture where belching is the normal way to compliment the food*

Interpretation: _____

_____

4. Someone makes the OK gesture at you. How would this be interpreted:

    ❂ *by someone in whose culture this gesture is obscene*

    Interpretation: _____

    _____

    ❂ *by someone in whose culture this gesture has romantic connotations*

    Interpretation: _____

    _____

5. A woman carries a heavy pile of wood on her back while her husband walks in front of her carrying nothing. How would this be interpreted:

    ❂ *by someone from a culture where women are proud of their strength and ability to work hard*

    Interpretation: _____

    _____

—INSIGHT—

A given behavior has no built-in meaning; it means whatever the observer decides it means.

6. A male guest helps a hostess carry dirty dishes into the kitchen. How would this act be interpreted:

    ❂ *by men from a culture where men never clean up after a meal*

    Interpretation: _____

    _____

I believe that participant observation is more than a research methodology. It is a way of being, especially suited to a world of change.

—**Mary Catherine Bateson**

✿ *by the hostess from that same culture*

Interpretation: _____

_____

7. A young man and a young woman are kissing each other while seated on a park bench. How would this act be interpreted:

✿ *by someone from a culture where men and women never touch in public*

Interpretation: _____

_____

8. While taking an exam, a student copies from the paper of another student. How would this act be interpreted:

✿ *by someone from a culture where exams are not fair and are designed to eliminate students at various stages of the education system*

Interpretation: _____

_____

✿ *by someone from a culture where it is shameful not to help your friend if you are able to*

Interpretation: _____

_____

1.10—DEFINING CULTURE ✍

Reading through this chapter, you notice a number of definitions of culture presented in the form of short quotations in the margins. Take a minute to reread these quotations and then note, in the spaces below, any idea, concept, or key word that is repeated more than once. Assembling these recurring phrases gives you a good working definition of culture.

1. _____

2. _____

3. _____

4. _____

5. _____

6. _____

7. _____

8. _____

[For one possible list, see page 233.]

—INSIGHT—

While culture has many definitions, most observers agree on certain fundamental characteristics.

INTRODUCING JAN—
AN ANALYSIS ॐ

Now that you have completed the activities in this chapter, look again at Exercise 1.1, the excerpt from Jan's journal. In light of what you have read in this chapter, do you find other passages you want to mark as questionable or inaccurate, or passages you underlined previously that now strike you as acceptable? Mark the text as necessary and then continue reading.

The purpose of these introductory excerpts from the writings of PCV Jan is to teach you about culture and cultural differences through the "actual" experiences—and in particular, the mistakes—of a typical Peace Corps Volunteer. For this technique to work, and especially for these lessons to have maximum impact, you are presented with more of Jan's errors than her triumphs. If Jan's experiences leave you with the notion that the Peace Corps experience is nothing more than a steady progression of cultural "faux pas", misunderstandings, and misinterpretations, remember that you haven't seen all the letters and journal entries Jan wrote that contained *no* cultural mistakes.

Jan will do fine. And so will you.

Paragraphs 1 & 2—

Jan is at the beginning of a dynamic process—getting to know how she, as an American, fits in with another culture. In this excerpt, she is full of enthusiasm, delighted with people's kindness, and understandably uncritical of the few host country nationals she has met. Nevertheless, she is right to listen to her host mother and keep an eye open for "bad people," even though she hasn't met any—yet.

Paragraphs 3 & 4—

At this stage, she is relieved to see that people "aren't as different as I thought they would be." Recognizing similarities (universal behaviors) is reassuring for anyone beginning a new adventure in a new country.

She is not taking her surroundings for granted, however. She is already experiencing some of the contradictions of living in a new culture, and she is conscious of the potential for disaster or for shocking people. She may have made a few cultural "faux pas," but no one may have told her so, not wanting to embarrass her. On the one hand, the people in the restaurant behaved as they would "back home." On the other hand, she was shocked at the "casual cruelty" of seeing someone kick a dog. Recognizing her feelings and reactions is important, but was that kick really casual cruelty? It's possible that it was self-protection, not wanting to be infected by the bite of a diseased animal.

Her book of do's and don'ts has probably provided her with a useful security blanket for her first few days. For Jan to have a deep understanding of her host culture and her interactions with people around her, however, it will be important for her to go beneath the surface, and learn the reasons and the values behind the do's and don'ts.

Finally, when Jan says she recognizes "a lot of common behaviors," she may indeed recognize the behaviors, but she may not be interpreting them correctly. At this stage, she cannot have experienced the many ways these people may act differently from what she is accustomed to. Her world is full of common behaviors because for the moment, these are the only ones she can see.

Paragraph 5—

"I have a lot to learn," says Jan. Her openness to new experiences and her willingness to reflect on her learnings in her journal are signs that she has started out well.

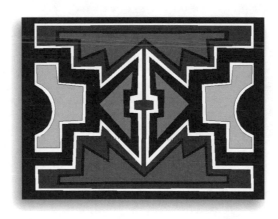

JOURNAL ENTRY 1

Use this space to react to or reflect on anything you might have learned in this chapter. Write whatever you like—notes to yourself, questions, feelings, fears, doubts. These are some questions you might want to consider: What did you learn about culture in this chapter that you didn't know before? What was the most important fact you learned? Do you now understand something about the local people that you didn't before? If answering these questions helps you, good; otherwise, ignore them. This space is for you.

FUNDAMENTALS OF CULTURE ✌
INTRODUCTION

Culture is a complex concept, with numerous dimensions and facets. This workbook presents and examines many of these, but singles out for more extensive treatment the four most important, the building blocks of culture:

I   THE CONCEPT OF THE SELF

II   PERSONAL VS. SOCIETAL OBLIGATIONS

III   THE CONCEPT OF TIME

IV   THE LOCUS OF CONTROL

The most significant ways in which cultures differ are in how they view and react to these four concepts. Not everything people do can be explained through them, but because they are so fundamental, they are often the source of or ultimate reason behind a wide range of thought and behavior. They give you a structure for thinking about and analyzing culture that can help you explain why host country people think and behave the way they do, and why you think and behave the way you do.

Each of these concepts, with related activities, is presented in a separate section between the workbook's regular chapters. A final section contains an exercise that asks you to compare and contrast your personal views on these topics with those of your own and of the host culture.

To have your eyes widened and your organ of belief stretched, whilst remaining discreetly submissive, seems to me a faculty the [traveler] ought to cultivate. When you have submitted to looking about you discreetly and to observing with as little prejudice as possible, then you are in a proper state of mind to walk about and learn from what you see.

—Philip Glazebrook,
<u>*Journey to Kars*</u>

I
II
III
IV

FUNDAMENTALS OF CULTURE I
THE CONCEPT OF THE SELF ✍

This exercise introduces the first of the four fundamentals of culture: the concept of the self. The two poles of this concept, individualism and collectivism, are defined and explored in the activity immediately following this one.

1.1—SHARING THE REWARDS ✍

For six weeks, you and the three other people in your division have been working on an important special project. Now the work is done and the four of you have been awarded a cash prize of $20,000. How should this money be distributed? In answering this question, you may find the following information useful:

1. Person A did 25% of the work.
2. Person B did 40% of the work.
3. Person C did 25% of the work.
4. Person D did 10% of the work.

In the underlined blank spaces below, write the cash prize you think each person should receive:

Person A $ _____

Person B $ _____

Person C $ _____

Person D $ _____

How did you reach your decision?

_____

_____

Now turn to page 234 to see how the same team would often be rewarded in a collectivist culture, and a brief discussion of why.

I.2—THE CONCEPT OF SELF—
INDIVIDUALISM & COLLECTIVISM ✍

You had a taste of what the concept of self entails in the previous activity, "Sharing the Rewards." Here you are given a general description of the two poles of this dimension, individualism and collectivism,* and asked to assign a list of behaviors to one side or the other. The two concepts are described briefly below. While no culture is exclusively individualist or collective—not to mention individuals within each type—most tend to be *more* one than the other.

Individualist—

The individual identifies primarily with self, with the needs of the individual being satisfied before those of the group. Looking after and taking care of oneself, being self-sufficient, guarantees the well being of the group. Independence and self-reliance are greatly stressed and valued. In general, people tend to distance themselves psychologically and emotionally from each other. One may *choose* to join groups, but group membership is not essential to one's identity or success. Individualist characteristics are often associated with men and people in urban settings.

Collectivist—

One's identity is in large part a function of one's membership and role in a group, e.g., the family or work team. The survival and success of the group ensures the well-being of the individual, so that by considering the needs and feelings of others, one protects oneself. Harmony and the interdependence of group members are stressed and valued. Group members are relatively close psychologically and emotionally, but distant toward nongroup members. Collectivist characteristics are often associated with women and people in rural settings.

Koreans were Confucian and therefore lived their lives according to the five Confucian relationships, while I lived my own life pretty much according to the personal pronoun "I."

— PCV Korea

Based on concepts developed by Triandis, <u>The analysis of subjective culture</u>, NY, Wiley-Interscience, 1972; Edward T. Hall, <u>The Silent Language</u>, Anchor-Doubleday, 1959; and Geert Hofstede, <u>Culture's Consequences,</u> Sage Publications, CA, 1980.

Now look at the list of behaviors or characteristics given below. If you decide the statement is *more likely* to apply to people living in an individualist culture, write "I" in the underlined blank space; if you think it is characteristic of a collectivist culture, write "C."

CHARACTERISTICS & BEHAVIORS

1. ____ People answer the phone by giving the name of the organization.

2. ____ People give cocktail parties.

3. ____ *Inter*group rivalry is strong.

4. ____ Employee-of-the-year awards are offered.

5. ____ People adhere to tradition.

6. ____ People are promoted based on production and results.

7. ____ Contracts in business are used frequently.

8. ____ There is a need for autonomy.

9. ____ People change jobs frequently.

10. ____ People believe that conflict clears the air.

11. ____ There is a need for affiliation.

12. ____ Short-term relationships are common.

13. ____ It's okay to stand out.

14. ____ Face saving is important.

15. ____ It's common for mothers to ask their preschoolers what they want to wear today.

16. ____ Self-help books are popular.

17. ____ Decisions are made by consensus.

18. ____ The language has one word for mother's brother, another for father's brother.

19. ____ Marriages are arranged.

20. ____ People have potluck dinners.

[For suggested answers, see page 234.]

—INSIGHT—

The concept of personal identity differs greatly from culture to culture.

THE ELECTRICIAN

The electrician turned out to be a young newlywed who lived just down the street. He showed up at my door late one afternoon with a screwdriver and a roll of electrical tape, and started taking things apart. That evening he could not find or fix the flaw, but he came back early the next day. When he was done I asked him, "How much do I owe you?"

The reply was standard. "Nothing. Just your thanks." No money. No goods in trade. Not even a beer or a soda. This is something I have experienced many times here in Alubaren, and it always leaves me stumped. Doesn't he realize what he just did for me is considered work? Doesn't he know that his time and effort have value? Doesn't he need every penny he can get to provide for his new wife and baby?

I think over some of the other times when I've experienced this same phenomenon: the bus driver who hauled my furniture over from the next village when the Volunteer there left; the seamstress who took in the waist of my shorts; the carpenter who carried my new bookshelf down the mountainside on his back. And there are more. What is it with all of these people who are so kind and do so much for me but never accept any payment or ask for anything in return? Is it because I'm the "gringa," an outsider, and they want to give a good impression of their people and their country?

That's what I thought at first, but now I've been in Alubaren long enough to have a truer perspective on how things work here. It's their sense of community, the great importance they attach to looking after each other. There's something very special about a place where the primary value placed on goods and services is the people's regard for one another.

—*PCV Honduras*

I feel my neighbors are rude, coming and asking for things from my garden. They believe I'm selfish keeping my first harvest to myself.

—*PCV Fiji*

I.3—SCORE YOURSELF—
INDIVIDUALIST OR COLLECTIVIST

Having become familiar with the two poles of this concept in the previous exercise, you now have a chance to think of your own behavior in the context of this important cultural dimension. Before reading further, take a moment to decide whether you think of yourself as more individualist or collectivist.

Below are a number of paired statements. Read each pair (a. and b.) and circle the one that best describes the action you would take or the way you feel about the particular topic. Please choose one or the other even if you think both are true. Try to be as honest as you can by answering quickly and not analyzing your response.

I had more than one Senegalese friend who owned only two pairs of pants but gave one away to someone whose only pair had become too ragged to be decent.

—PCV Senegal

1a. Managers should be hired from within the organization, based mainly on their seniority.

1b. Managers should be hired on the basis of the skills they have and previous experience in similar jobs.

2a. It takes a long time to make a new friend.

2b. Friends can be made relatively quickly.

3a. If I took a job with a new company, I would expect my old employer to wish me well.

3b. If I took a job with a new company, I would be afraid that my employer might lose face.

4a. I expect people to judge me by my achievements.

4b. I expect people to judge me by my affiliations.

5a. Before making a decision, it is best to make sure everyone agrees with it.

5b. Before making a decision, you should get at least half of the people to agree with it.

6a. I am embarrassed by individual recognition.

6b. If I do a good job, I feel I have earned individual recognition.

7a. Making sure people don't lose face is more important than always being completely honest.

7b. Being straight with people is always best in the end.

8a. If my brother or sister did wrong, I would admit this to other people.

8b. If my brother or sister did wrong, I would defend them to other people.

9a. Confrontation is sometimes necessary to clear the air.

9b. Confrontation almost always causes more problems than it solves.

10a. In the end, you can always rely on other people.

10b. In the end, you can only rely on yourself.

Now that you have made your selections, turn to page 235 for results, and then calculate whether you came out more on the individualist or collectivist side. Is your score here consistent with your self-concept?

Keep in mind that this exercise is not scientific. Most of the paired statements are taken out of context; you might select one alternative in one set of circumstances and the opposite in another. The exercise, however, has exposed you to some alternative behaviors and ways of thinking that you might want to consider as you continue your Peace Corps experience.

—INSIGHT—

Culture influences whether you act more like an individualist or a collectivist.

*This independence is something
Guineans cannot understand.
Making it on your own is not
valued.*

—PCV Guinea Bissau.

I.4—PLEASED TO MEET YOU ✍

One way in which people suggest whether they are more individualist or collectivist is in how they introduce themselves. The idea of an introduction, of course, is to establish who you are, to fix your identity. Think for a moment what you usually say about yourself when you meet someone you don't know, or what the other person usually asks about you. How do you introduce yourself to a group, before giving a presentation? Write down two or three things you would mention about yourself.

Now listen to a few host country people when they introduce themselves. What information do they provide? What do other people ask them? What do they say when introducing themselves to a group before giving a presentation? In the space below, write what you've noticed, and then reflect on any differences between what these people say and what people in the U.S. would say.

CHAPTER TWO ✌
AMERICAN CULTURE
AND AMERICAN DIVERSITY

The essence of cross-cultural understanding is knowing how your own culture is both similar to and different from the local or "target" culture. For this reason, those who pursue cross-cultural knowledge must sooner or later turn their gaze on themselves. People from other cultures, after all, aren't different by nature, but only different *in relation to* a particular standard they're being measured against. To even see those differences, therefore, you have to examine that standard. In the case of the Peace Corps, that standard is the American culture that Volunteers come from. This chapter contains a series of activities designed to reveal that American culture.

You might wonder why people from the United States would need to have their culture revealed to them—isn't it pretty obvious?—but the fact is that people *from* a culture, as you learned in Chapter 1, are in many ways the least able to see it. They embody the culture, of course, but they would in fact have to get out of that body if they wanted to see what it looked like. In that sense, you might want to think of this chapter as an out-of-body experience, courtesy of Peace Corps training.

As was noted earlier, no one American is quite like any other American, but a handful of core values and beliefs do underlie and permeate the national culture. These values and beliefs don't apply across the board in every situation, and we may, on occasion, even act in ways that directly contradict or flaunt them, but they are still at the heart of our cultural ethos. It is some of these beliefs, with the characteristic behaviors that come from them, that are the focus of this chapter.

Remember as you do these exercises that whether or not you personally can identify with or believe in the typical American being constructed here, this is the image that many host country people have of Americans.

It is shocking for me to see how the father and mother in America kick their own children out when they become eighteen years of age. The most surprising thing about it all is that the young people do not seem to mind or think it is too cruel to be thrown out of their own family but accept it as the natural and normal way of behaving.

—HCN from Cameroon, in Robert Kohls & John Knight, Developing Intercultural Awareness

2.1—DEAR TODD ✍

It's time to catch up with Jan, who is now nearing the end of her training program and about to take up her Peace Corps assignment. At right is a letter Jan has written to her friend Todd back in the United States. In her letter, Jan makes a number of statements that reflect deeply held, characteristic American values or cultural assumptions. Underline any statements of this kind you can identify and then go on to the rest of the activities in this chapter.

Dear Todd,

1. *Please excuse me for not answering your letter sooner, but we're nearing the end of our training program here and life is quite busy as I prepare to take up my assignment. After all these months of anticipating—years, if you count all the time I've been thinking about joining the Peace Corps—it's finally going to happen: I'm going to walk into a village, find a place to live, and start saving the world. Well, maybe not the <u>entire</u> world. And maybe not on the first day. But I'll do my best.*

2. *Actually, if we have learned anything during this training—and we have learned a lot—it's to have realistic expectations of what we can actually accomplish here. Some of us, and I count myself among this group, were probably a bit ambitious about our work and the difference we could make, but I'm much more grounded in reality now. Thank goodness.*

3. *I know that making changes and improvements takes time, so I don't expect to see any results for the first few months. You've got to get people to trust you, after all, but once they do, then you can start to have influence. I think that once they're aware of my training and experience in the field, I'm bound to become more credible to them. People are basically well-intentioned, after all. You just have to give them time and the benefit of the doubt.*

4. *I know there will be obstacles, but I also know I'll be able to overcome them. If you put your mind to something, and it's something that means as much to you as this does to me, then nothing can stop you. I can give you an example of this from a recent incident here at the training program. We [trainees] wanted to set up a little co-op inside the training center, where we could buy soft drinks, snacks, etc., because the closest store is about half an hour from here, and we don't have time to go there and back on our breaks. When we approached the people who run this place, they said the stores in town wouldn't sell directly to us but only to the training center, i.e., to them, and they would arrange it for us. But we told them we wanted to do all the talking and arranging ourselves, so we could practice using the language in real situations and probably have a few cross-cultural experiences along the way. They said nothing like that had ever been done before and they didn't think it was a good idea.*

(continued)

I'm not English. I'm American. We see all things as possible.

—Norman Mailer,
The <u>Times</u>
of London

5. *But I wasn't willing to give up so soon, so I approached some merchants in town. And found there was no problem at all! They were happy to sell to anyone, and they would give us a bulk discount! It's a small example, but it shows you that you don't have to take no for an answer, and that the way things have always been done doesn't have to be the way they're done hereafter.*

6. *Maybe I was lucky this time, but I think a positive attitude (along with my stubborn streak) can get you a long way.*

Well, there's a lot more I want to tell you, but it's time for class. You probably won't hear from me for two or three weeks now, until I get moved and set up in my town. But don't use that as an excuse for not writing! We LIVE for our mail around here.

Love,

Jan

2.2—THE THINGS WE SAY— CULTURE IN CASUAL EXPRESSIONS ☙

PART ONE

A useful way to understand a culture is by examining the expressions people use in everyday conversation. These common expressions, after all, reflect what most people in a given society believe in or value. What cultural value or belief do the following expressions reveal? Write your response in the space provided. The first group of expressions is done for you.

1. He thinks he's better than so and so.
2. She's always putting on airs.
3. That person should be cut down to size.
4. It's gone to his head.

Value/belief: Egalitarianism

1. Talk is cheap.
2. Put your money where your mouth is.
3. He's all talk and no action.

Value/belief: _____

4. She's always beating around the bush.
5. Tell it like it is.
6. Straight talk, straight answer, straight shooter.

Value/belief: _____

7. She did something with her life.
8. Nice guys finish last.

Value/belief: _____

The people who are not pleased with America must be those whose sympathies are fossilized or whose eyes have no power of observation. Such delightful and entertaining schemes for hoodwinking nature you never saw, such ingenuities for beating the terrible forces of the seasons, such daring inventions.

—*Edmond Gosse*
The Life and Letters of Sir Edmond Gosse, 1884

9. Every cloud has a silver lining.
10. Look on the bright side.
11. Tomorrow is another day.

   Value/belief: _____

12. Where there's a will there's a way.

   Value/belief: _____

13. Stand on your own two feet.

   Value/belief: _____

14. Don't judge a book by its cover.
15. All that glitters isn't gold.

   Value/belief: _____

16. Nothing ventured, nothing gained.

   Value/belief: _____

All kinds of tourists are fair game for [con artists] but Americans seem their favorite targets, not just because of their careless ways with money and instinctive generosity, but also their non-European innocence about the viler dimensions of human nature...

—Paul Fussell,
Abroad

[For suggested answers, see page 235.]

Can you think of other common expressions, ones you use yourself or that are common in your family? Write them below and then list the value or belief they represent.

1. _____

   Value:

2. _____

   Value:

3. _____

   Value:

Informant Activity

PART TWO

Just as expressions common in the U.S. reveal aspects of the national culture, so do host country espressions reveal certain host country values or beliefs. Using a host country informant or a PCV who knows the local culture well, try to come up with at least five common host country expressions, and then identify the cultural belief behind them. You may use proverbs, if you like, but in many cases, you may find that the same proverb exists in one form or another in many cultures, so that the value it reveals is probably universal and not specific to your host country.

1. _____

   Value/belief:

2. _____

   Value/belief:

3. _____

   Value/belief:

—INSIGHT—

Common expressions
become common
because they reflect
core cultural values.

4. _____

   Value/belief:

5. _____

   Value/belief:

I was so surprised and confused when, on leaving Whittier Hall, the provost, in person, held the door for me in order to let me pass. I was so confused that I could not find the words to express my gratefulness, and I almost fell on my knees as I would certainly do back home.

A man who is by far my superior is holding the door for me, a mere student and a nobody.

—A visitor from Indonesia in John Fieg & John Blair, There Is A Difference

Informant Activity

2.3—THIRTEEN CULTURAL CATEGORIES— AMERICAN AND HOST COUNTRY VIEWS COMPARED

This activity looks at 13 categories or aspects of culture and compare the typical American position on these matters with that of your host country. In each case, the American view has been summarized and illustrated for you as adapted from the work of several intercultural experts including Edward Stewart, Milton Bennett, Gary Althen * and several authors in the Interact series from Intercultural Press. It is your task to get together with an informant, either a host country national or someone else who knows the host culture well, and try to construct the host country position. You may, if you wish, do this activity with another trainee. After you have made notes on or constructed the host country position, try to get together with other trainees in your group and compare observations.

1. ATTITUDE TOWARDS AGE

- ✪ Emphasize physical beauty and youth.
- ✪ Fire older people to hire younger people for less money.
- ✪ Judge a worker's worth based on production, not seniority.

American View—The American emphasis on concrete achievements and "doing" means that age is not highly valued, for the older you are the less you can accomplish. Age is also suspect because new is usually better in American culture, and the elderly are generally out of touch with what's new.

Host Country View:

*Based on concepts developed by Edward Stewart and Milton Bennett, American Cultural Patterns, Intercultural Press, Yarmouth, ME, 1991; Gary Althen, American Ways, Intercultural Press, Yarmouth, ME, 1981.

2. CONCEPT OF FATE AND DESTINY

- ✪ You can be whatever you want to be.
- ✪ Where there's a will there's a way.
- ✪ The American dream is rags-to-riches.

American View—The concept of self-determination negates much of the influence of fate and destiny. Parents tell their children they can be whatever they want to be when they grow up. There are few givens in life, and people have little sense of external limits. Lack of success is their own fault.

Host Country View:

For me, there was only one place to go if I couldn't live in my own country: America. It is a country of immigrants. There is such tolerance for the foreign and unfamiliar. America continues to amaze me.

—Milosc Forman

3. VIEW OF HUMAN NATURE

- ✪ Courts consider a person innocent until he/she is proven guilty.
- ✪ People should be given the benefit of the doubt.
- ✪ If left alone, people will do the right thing.
- ✪ We need to discover how a vicious killer "went wrong."

American View—People are considered basically and inherently good. If someone does an evil deed, we look for the explanation, for the reason why the person turned bad. People can and should be trusted; and we are fairly open to strangers, and willing to accept them.

Host Country View:

4. ATTITUDE TOWARDS CHANGE

- ✪ New is better.
- ✪ A better way can always be found; things can always be improved upon.
- ✪ Just because we've always done it that way doesn't make it right.

American View—Change is considered positive, probably because Americans believe in the march of progress and the pursuit of perfection. Improvements will always move us closer and closer to perfection. Traditions can be a guide, but they are not inherently superior.

Host Country View:

5. ATTITUDE TOWARDS TAKING RISKS

- ✪ A low level of personal savings is typical.
- ✪ You can always start over.
- ✪ Nothing ventured, nothing gained.
- ✪ A high level of personal bankruptcies is common.

American View—There will always be enough opportunity to go around, so taking risks, involves no real danger. For the truly ambitious, failure is only temporary. Experimentation, trial and error are important ways to learn or to improve your product or service.

Host Country View:

6. CONCEPT OF SUFFERING AND MISFORTUNE

✪ People rush to cheer up a friend who's depressed.

✪ If you're unhappy, take a pill or see a psychiatrist.

✪ Be happy.

American View—Because we are ultimately in control of our lives and destiny, we have no excuse for unhappiness nor misfortune. If you are suffering or unhappy, then just do whatever it takes to be happy again. If you're depressed, it's because you have chosen to be.

Host Country View:

7. CONCEPT OF FACE

✪ It's important to tell it like it is, be straight with people.

✪ Confrontation is sometimes necessary to clear the air.

✪ Honesty is the best policy.

American View—In individualist cultures, no premium is put on saving face because people can take care of themselves. What other people think is not so crucial to survival or success. We can say what we think without worrying about hurting people's feelings, and we likewise appreciate directness.

Host Country View:

You have to be very subservient to people: "Ma'am, can I take your bag?" "Can I do this?" Being subservient to people made me very resentful.

—Supermarket box boy in Working *by Studs Terkel*

8. SOURCE OF SELF ESTEEM/SELF WORTH

- People judge you by how much money you make.
- First question at a party is, "What do you do?"
- Material possessions are a measure of success.

American View—In an individualist culture, you are what you've achieved; that is, you create your own worth rather than receiving it by virtue of birth, position, seniority, or longevity. Your self-esteem comes from what you have done to *earn* self-esteem.

Host Country View:

9. CONCEPT OF EQUALITY

- People try to treat everyone the same.
- While jogging, the President stops at McDonald's for morning coffee.
- Putting on airs is frowned upon.

American View—In a strong reaction to the repressive class structure in Europe, Americans created a culture virtually built around egalitarianism: the notion that no one is superior to anyone else because of birth, power, fame, or wealth. We are not all the same, but we are all of equal value.

Host Country View:

10. Attitude Towards Formality

- ✪ Telling someone to help themselves to what's in the refrigerator is common.
- ✪ Using first names with people you've just met is fine.
- ✪ Using titles like "Dr". for someone with a Ph.D. is presumptuous.

American View—Because of the strong egalitarian ethos, Americans tend to be casual and informal in social and professional interactions. Informality is also more necessary in a mobile society where people are always meeting new people. We don't stand on ceremony, nor use titles or rank in addressing each other.

Host Country View:

Bold Talent shook his head. How like children the Americans were, with their pranks and easy warmth. Men who offered their hands for strangers to shake, ladies who sat and chatted at dinner with gentlemen they had never seen before, children who threw snowballs at adults no matter what their station. He would miss them.

—Bette Bao Lord,
Spring Moon

11. Degree of Realism

- ✪ Things will get better.
- ✪ Bad things happen for a reason.
- ✪ It can't get any worse.
- ✪ Tag line of fairy tales: "They lived happily ever after."

American View—Largely because of the notion that the individual is in control, Americans are generally optimistic. We don't see things the way they are, but as better than they are, particularly if they're not so good. We feel it's important to be positive and that there is no reason not to be.

Host Country View:

12. Attitude Towards Doing

- Doing is preferred over talking.
- The absent-minded professor, the ivory tower reflect anti-intellectualism.
- Be practical.
- Arts are an adornment of life but not central to it.

American View—Individuals survive because they get things done, generally on their own. Words and talk are suspect and cheap; they don't put food on the table or a roof over your head. Pursuits not directly related to the creation of concrete results, e.g., academia, the arts, are less highly valued. What is practical and pragmatic is favored over what is beautiful and inspiring.

Host Country View:

—Insight—

Behaviors reflect deeply seated values and world views.

13. View of the Natural World

- Building dams to control rivers.
- Seeding clouds to produce rain.
- Erecting earthquake-proof buildings.
- Spending billions annually on weather prediction.

American View—The natural world is a kind of mechanism or machine that can be studied and known and whose workings can be predicted, manipulated, and ultimately controlled. It is not to be feared.

Host Country View:

2.4—THINKING ABOUT MY JOB ✍

In the previous exercise, you discovered a number of differences in the way American and host country people view certain key topics. These differences are bound to show up now and again as you go about working at your Peace Corps assignment. Below are five of the categories from the previous exercise, with examples of typical work-related problems. Read each incident and note what you would do.

1. ATTITUDE TOWARDS AGE

The American emphasis on achievements and doing means that age is to be feared and not respected; the older you are, the less you can do or contribute to society. Age is also suspect because new is usually better in American culture, and the elderly are generally out of touch with what is new.

Suppose you're a technical expert in crop rotation assigned to a co-op of village farmers. You discover they do not consult you or even pay much attention to you because they think you're too young to know what you're doing.

My response: _____

_____

2. ATTITUDE TOWARDS CHANGE

Change is considered positive, probably because Americans believe in the march of progress and the perfectability of man. Improvements will always move us closer and closer to perfection. Traditions can be a guide, but they are not inherently superior.

You want to introduce a new teaching technique to your colleagues. It is a faster and more efficient way of presenting certain concepts. When you approach them, they respond: "This is the way we have always been taught." You say, "But this is faster and more efficient." They say, "No doubt."

My response: _____

_____

Americans ignore history....The national myth is that of creativity and progress....They believe in the future as if it were a religion; they believe that there is nothing they cannot accomplish, that solutions wait somewhere for all problems, like brides.

—Frances Fitzgerald,
Fire in the Lake

3. CONCEPT OF EQUALITY

In a strong reaction to the repressive class structure in Europe, Americans created a culture built around egalitarianism: the notion that no one is inherently superior to anyone else because of birth, power, fame, or wealth. We are not all the same, but we are all of equal value.

It has turned cold the last few days and you feel sorry for the teaboy who is stationed just outside the entrance to your building. He doesn't seem to have any warm clothes and huddles over his charcoal fire to keep warm. You approach your boss and ask if you can tell the boy to move into the hallway out of the cold. "Certainly not," he replies. "This building is for faculty, not teaboys."

My response: _____

_____

4. ATTITUDE TOWARDS TAKING RISKS

There will always be enough opportunity to go around, so taking risks involves no real danger. For the truly ambitious, failure is only temporary. Experimentation, trial and error are important ways to learn or to improve your product or service.

You want to try a new way of filtering drinking water for the village. The environmental engineer asks you if this technique has been tried anywhere else in the country, to which you answer, "No. "And what if we fail?" he asks you. "Then we go back to the old way," you respond. "And what happens to my job?" he replies.

My response: _____

_____

5. VIEW OF THE NATURAL WORLD

> The natural world is a kind of mechanism or machine that can be studied and known and whose workings can be predicted, manipulated, and ultimately controlled. It is not to be feared.

Books need to be ordered now to arrive in time for the start of classes in the fall. You go to the head librarian to put in your request, and she asks you how you know how many students you're going to have. You don't of course, but you're projecting, based on previous class size. "It's better to wait," she says, "so we don't waste money buying extra books." You know that if you don't order now, you'll have to teach for several weeks without the books while you wait for them to arrive.

My response: _____

_____

[For suggested answers, see page 235.]

—INSIGHT—

Cultural differences are bound to show up in workplace interactions.

2.5—SOURCES OF AMERICAN CULTURE

In this exercise, you reexamine some of the American values you have identified thus far, trying to understand where they come from. While it is useful to know *what* it is Americans value and believe in, it is also helpful to know *why* they believe what they do—to understand that our values and beliefs are a result of our national experience. Once you understand this fact about your own country's culture, you can begin to appreciate that it must be true of your host country as well.

Below are four defining features of the people who came to the United States, followed by a numbered list of American traits, many of which you have come across earlier in this chapter. Place the number of the trait in the space beneath the defining feature/s you feel is the likely source of or reason behind the trait. An example from the list of traits is given for each of them. (Please note that these features describe the people who originally settled the United States and may not describe many Americans of today.)

DEFINING FEATURES

PROTESTANTISM—

A strong work ethic—work is intrinsically good—and the notion of predestination, that salvation is apparent through worldly success.

7. The cult of celebrities; biographies of the rich and famous.

AMERICAN GEOGRAPHY—

The frontier, unlimited resources and opportunity, isolation, sparse population, distance from Europe.

1. Limited sense of fatalism, of accepting things as they are.

ESCAPE FROM REPRESSION—

From religious and economic repression and rigid class system and social stratification.

2. Tolerance for differences.

But the firemen; you actually see them produce. I used to work in a bank. You know, it's just paper. It's not real. Nine to five and it's s___. You're lookin' at numbers. But now I can look back and say, "I helped put out a fire. I helped save somebody." It shows something I did on this earth.

—Tom Patrick, fireman, in Studs Terkel, Working

THE NATURE OF THE AMERICAN IMMIGRANT—

Out of the mainstream in home country, dissatisfied with lot in life, willing to take risks, adventuresome.

8. Little fear of failure.

The happy ending is our national belief.

—Mary McCarthy

TRAITS

1. Limited sense of fatalism, of accepting things as they are
2. Tolerance for differences
3. Historic low level of savings
4. Self-reliance
5. A president, not a king
6. Informality: "Call me Bob."
7. The cult of celebrities; biographies of the rich and famous
8. Little fear of failure
9. Modest limits on immigration
10. Acceptance of criticism or disagreement with the boss or authority figures
11. Emphasis on achievement
12. Checks and balances in the U.S. Constitution
13. Identification with work or job
14. Idea of a second chance, of starting over
15. Minimal supervision from bosses
16. Egalitarianism
17. Virtue of change, of newness
18. Rags to riches syndrome: the self-made man or woman
19. Waste: the disposable society; little conservation of resources
20. Frequent job and career changes
21. Big cars, big houses, sprawling malls
22. Desire to be own boss, self-employed
23. Optimism
24. Mobile society; frequency with which people move

—INSIGHT—

Many American traits are the direct result either of our geography or of the nature of the immigrants who first settled our country.

[For suggested answers, see page 236.]

2.6—HOW NON-AMERICANS SEE AMERICANS ✎

PART ONE

In this two-part activity, you look at how Americans are perceived by people from other cultures. Knowing how we come across can be helpful in understanding why foreigners react to us the way they sometimes do.

Newsweek magazine showed the list of qualities given below to people in six countries— Brazil, France, Great Britain, Japan, Mexico, and Germany—and asked them to pick those they associated most and least with Americans.

What do you think were the four qualities most associated with Americans?

1. _____   2. _____

3. _____   4. _____

What do you think were the four qualities least associated with Americans?

1. _____   2. _____

3. _____   4. _____

QUALITIES		
Decisive	Energetic	Honest
Industrious	Sexy	Self-indulgent
Sophisticated	Intelligent	Friendly
Greedy	Nationalistic	Inventive
Lazy	Rude	

[The survey results are on page 236.]

Informant Activity

PART TWO

In the second part of this activity, you need to get together with a host country national or a PCV to stand in as HCN and ask this person which of the qualities from Part One he/she associates most and least with Americans. Write the answers in the spaces provided below. Then ask your informant why he/she selected those particular qualities.

What qualities do you associate <u>most</u> with Americans?

1. _____   3. _____

2. _____

What qualities do you associate <u>least</u> with Americans?

1. _____   3. _____

2. _____

—INSIGHT —

Host country nationals may have a number of preconceptions about Americans.

2.7—LEARNING ABOUT AMERICA ✐

Living in another culture can make you more aware of your own culture. In the space below, name two or three characteristics of American life or of Americans that you did not realize before you came here. How did you come to these realizations?

2.8—NOW WHAT?
DIVERSITY CRITICAL INCIDENTS ✺

Trainees and Volunteers who come from minority or distinctive populations in the United States are often faced with special issues in the Peace Corps. Some of these issues are illustrated in the incidents presented below. After reading each incident, describe what you would do if you had this experience, or what you would advise if it happened to someone you knew who came to you for help.

COME WITH US

You are a strong Christian whose religious beliefs are an essential part of your identity. You have been posted in a country with an entirely different religious tradition. Recently, some of your closest friends at work have been pressuring you to attend one of their religious services and asking you if you would like to learn more about their religion. You have politely declined their invitations and would, in fact, feel uncomfortable attending one of these events. Now, one of these individuals, your counterpart at work, explains that he believes you are prejudiced against his religion. What do you say or do?

AREN'T YOU NORMAL?

You are a gay Volunteer serving in what you have heard is a somewhat homophobic country where unmarried young men regularly patronize prostitutes. For some time, your male colleagues at work have been pressuring you to "have fun" with them on their Friday night outings, but you have declined. Now one of them has asked you if you are "normal." What do you say or do?

Being an African American in Africa has its frustrations and rewards. I have been challenged to define my identity as a person of African descent and as an American. I had to come to terms with many personal issues, like my whiteness in the eyes of Africans and in my own eyes.

—PCV West Africa

NATIVE SPEAKER

You are a Volunteer of Hispanic background whose family is third-generation American. You do not speak Spanish and have a normal American accent. You teach English at a high school in your country. After you have been at your site one month, some of your students complain to the headmaster that they want a different teacher, someone who is a native speaker of English. What do you say or do?

HELP

You are a blind PCV. You are a self-sufficient individual and value your independence. You have adjusted well at your post, but you are concerned about all the "help" you are getting from host country friends and colleagues. It is apparent that many HCNs regard people with disabilities as being unable to function without considerable assistance from those around them. At work and out in public, you are being helped to do all manner of things you are quite capable of doing on your own. While you appreciate people's concern, you are frustrated by being the focus of so much attention and support. What can you do or say to change this dynamic?

DOUBT

You are an African American serving in a country where prejudice against Black people is traditional. At a teacher training college, you notice that the students you are assigned to teach do not seem to respect you. One day, as you are explaining a concept, one of the students raises her hand and asks a question, "Are Black people allowed to go to college in the United States?" What do you say?

MANUAL LABOR

You are an older Volunteer in excellent physical condition. You work as project manager on a school construction site. You are not especially impressed with the work of some of the subcontractors, especially the carpenters, and have on several occasions tried to show them how to do their work better. But every time you try to climb on the building or do any manual work, your assistant steps in and says it's not appropriate for you, an older man and the project manager, to do strenuous physical labor. He says you will lose the respect of the real manual laborers if you continue to do this work. Now what?

They had too much energy, even for Americans.

—John LeCarre

YOUR OWN STORY

You may have already had your own critical incident in country. Reflect on it here and note down any lesson you learned or advice you would give someone else who had the same experience.

[For brief notes on these incidents, turn to page 236.]

2.9—ON BEING DIFFERENT 🖋

Whatever your background, you're not like the host country nationals in the place where you serve. All of us have been in situations before where we were different, and we adjusted our behavior accordingly. Think of how you behaved or spoke on such occasions and write your observations here.

[For suggestions, see page 237.]

2.10—PARTING ADVICE ✍

As you look back on what you've learned or been reminded of about the United States in this chapter, what stands out? Suppose you are at the airport one day and you meet a host country friend who's about to depart for a two-year stay in the United States. Your friend asks you to "tell me about America." You've got time to make three points about your culture. What would you tell your friend? (Feel free to draw your ideas instead.) When you have finished, show your list or drawings to at least one other member of your group and compare your answers.

1.

2.

3.

The American seems very explicit; he wants a Yes or No. If someone tries to speak figuratively, the American is confused.

—HCN from Ethiopia in John Fieg & John Blair, There Is A Difference

INTERVIEW WITH A PCV

Friend:	Were there any real surprises?
Peace Corps Volunteer:	Not really. I mean, you're not prepared for every little thing, for all the particulars. But you know the people are going to be different, so you expect that. You may not know all the ways they're going to surprise you, but you do know you're going to be surprised when you go to a foreign culture.
Friend:	How did the host country people react to you?
PCV:	It's funny you should ask that, because that *was* surprising.
Friend:	What do you mean?
PCV:	Well, we thought we were prepared for that, but we weren't. After all, if you go in knowing these people aren't like you, then of course you also know that you aren't like them. But we had trouble believing that they found us strange sometimes. Doesn't make sense, does it?
Friend:	So it's easy to accept that other people might be strange but hard to believe you could be?
PCV:	That's what I experienced, anyway.
Friend:	I wonder why.
PCV:	I think it has to be that while *you* are actually having the experience of their strangeness, *they* are the ones having the experience of yours. You never really experience yourself as strange, of course, so it just doesn't seem real. You know it must be, but you have to take their word for it.
Friend:	So you think Volunteers go around never quite convinced that the local people don't always understand them?
PCV:	If you listen to some of the complaints PCVs make, I think that's at the bottom of a lot of them.

DEAR TODD—AN ANALYSIS

Now that you've completed this chapter, read Jan's letter to Todd again and note any examples of typical American attitudes or values; then continue reading below.

Paragraphs 1 & 2—
Jan's opening is encouraging. She has perspective on herself and what she can accomplish in country. Even more hopeful, she has a good sense of humor and is able to laugh at herself.

Paragraph 3—
Jan's talk about making improvements reflects a basic American assumption: that things can always be better. Some cultures may not be quite so optimistic. While she's right about needing to be trusted before you can expect anyone to listen to you, it may take more than "training and experience in the field" to impress people. What also establishes credibility in many cultures are age, gender, who you know, and what important people think of you or your ideas. Jan may also be off track when she says that people are well-intentioned and should be given the benefit of the doubt. Not all cultures believe that human nature is basically good or that people can automatically be trusted; some cultures think just the opposite.

Paragraphs 4 & 5—
Jan's belief that she will be able to overcome obstacles reflects her basic optimism. There's nothing wrong with optimism, but it doesn't always reflect reality, nor would people in many cultures believe that all you have to do is put your mind to something, and then it will happen. Jan's story is likewise instructive. It does demonstrate that you don't always have to take no for an answer, but she may not be aware of all that was happening in this incident. It's entirely possible that the people who ran the training center knew quite well that merchants would sell to anyone— What merchant wouldn't?—and the real reason they discouraged Jan and company was because they themselves wanted to buy the merchandise, make a small profit, and be loyal to the people they knew. It was not necessarily wrong for Jan to persist, but by following Jan's example, going outside the system and doing what "has never been done before," you are normally taking a risk. Usually things are done the way they are for a *reason*, and you should probably learn that reason before you proceed. In this case, the reason was rather mundane and Jan has probably not done any damage. But imagine that she was at her workplace and did something similar, thereby alienating an important local figure.

Paragraph 6—
"A positive attitude" is Jan's optimism showing through again. Some cultures would say it's more important to have a realistic attitude.

In England, if something goes wrong—say, if one finds a skunk in the garden, he writes to the family lawyer who proceeds to take the proper measures; whereas in America you telephone the fire department. Each response satisfies a characteristic need: In the English, love of order and legalistic procedure; and here in America what you like is something vivid and swift.

—A.N Whitehead

JOURNAL ENTRY 2

In this chapter, you've had a chance to reflect on and analyze some of the differences between Americans and host country nationals. How has this process helped you to understand or explain anything you've seen or that has happened to you thus far in country? Did anything you learned surprise you? Do you have questions you wish to explore further?

FUNDAMENTALS OF CULTURE II
PERSONAL VS. SOCIETAL OBLIGATIONS ✑

This exercise introduces the second of the four fundamentals of culture: personal versus societal obligations, or the conflict between individual and social ethics. The two poles of this dimension, universalism and particularism, are defined and explored in the activity that immediately follows this one.

II.1—AN ACCIDENT ✑

You are riding in a car driven by a close friend when he hits a pedestrian. There are no other witnesses and the pedestrian is bruised but not badly hurt. The speed limit in this part of town is 20 miles an hour, but you happen to notice that your friend was driving 35. His lawyer tells you that if you will testify under oath that your friend was driving 20, he will suffer no serious consequences. (Adapted from Fons Trompenaars, *Riding the Waves of Culture*)

Before reading further, circle the "Yes" or "No" in answer to this question:

Would you testify that your friend
was driving 20 miles an hour?   Yes   No

| Percentage of Americans who said they would not: | 96% |
| Percentage of Venezuelans who said they would not: | 34% |

What do you think accounts for the great difference between Venezuelan and American percentages?

_____

_____

_____

—INSIGHT—

The responsibilities of friendship differ from culture to culture.

After writing your answer, turn to page 238 for a brief discussion.

II.2—PERSONAL AND SOCIETAL OBLIGATIONS— UNIVERSALISM & PARTICULARISM

As was suggested by the preceding activity, people struggle with how to balance obligations to family, friends, and colleagues on the one hand and to the wider society on the other. In cases where these obligations conflict, the people of different cultures often come down on different sides of this dichotomy.

The exercise that appears below helps you to define the two sides of this dimension of human experience—universalism and particularism.* No culture is exclusively universalist or particularist, but cultures do tend to be *more* one than the other, and while the attitudes of individuals in a given culture will vary, the focus here is on the culture as a whole. Brief descriptions of the two poles follow.

Universalism—
Certain absolutes apply across the board, regardless of circumstances or the particular situation. Wherever possible, you should try to apply the same rules to everyone in like situations. To be fair is to treat everyone alike and not make exceptions for family, friends, or members of your in-group. Where possible, you should lay your personal feelings aside and look at the situation objectively. While life isn't necessarily fair, we can make it more fair by treating people the same way.

Particularism—
How you behave in a given situation depends on the circumstances. You treat family, friends, and your in-group the best you can, and you let the rest of the world take care of itself. Their in-groups will protect them. There can't be absolutes because everything depends on whom you're dealing with. No one expects life to be fair. Exceptions will always be made for certain people.

Resting and gossiping under a tree, the medical aides would sometimes refuse treatment, saying the clinic was "closed for cleaning." It was a lie; no cleaning ever went on in that miserable mud-brick clinic. But having been appointed by relatives, the aides knew no work was required of them to keep their jobs.

—PCV Senegal

*Based on concepts developed by Fons Trompenaars, <u>Riding the Waves of Culture</u>, Irwin, NY 1994 and Charles Hampden-Turner and Fons Trompenaars, <u>The Seven Cultures of Capitalism</u>, Doubleday Currency, 1993.

In the following exercise, circle the statement that does not belong in the group of four, either because it reflects a universalist attitude and all the others are particularist, or vice versa:

1. Objectivity, not letting personal feelings affect decision making, is possible and desirable.
2. A deal is a deal, whatever happens.
3. Principles have to get bent once in a while.
4. The law is the law.

1. You don't compromise on principles.
2. Friends expect preferential treatment.
3. Subjectivity is the rule.
4. The logic of the heart is what counts.

1. People tend to hire friends and associates.
2. Consistency is desirable and possible.
3. Logic of the head is important.
4. Exceptions to the rule should be minimized.

1. Friends protect friends.
2. Life is neat, not messy.
3. Written contracts are not necessary.
4. This attitude is more consistent with collectivism.

1. Situational ethics are the norm.
2. A deal is a deal, until circumstances change.
3. Deals are made on the basis of personal relationships.
4. Justice is blind.

[For suggested answers, see page 238.]

—INSIGHT—

Cultures differ on how they distinguish between obligations to in-group and out-group members.

ERNIE

Ernie, Harry, Gordon, and I commuted for years together in the 1980s. Ernie, we found out, spoke Czech before he spoke English, but he had never set foot outside America. He and his brother and sister grew up in the Czech-speaking Valach family in Montana, his father having immigrated to the States in 1910.

I called Ernie excitedly when I found out the Peace Corps was assigning me to what was then Czechoslovakia. He supplied me with a list of his Czech first cousins, none of whom he'd ever met or spoken to, and the name of the village where his father was born, in 1892.

I went to that village one cool, sunny day. When I got off the bus I spotted the town hall. In Czech, I explained to the competent-looking, wide-eyed woman and young man in jeans that I had a friend in Oregon whose father was born in Rostin and had left for the United States as a young man. I timidly added that I was looking for my friend's cousin, Antonin.

It turned out the man in jeans was the mayor; he knew cousin Antonin and everyone else in town. We went to the family cottage on the outskirts of the village. The family was a bit surprised to see the mayor—and even more surprised when he explained I was from Oregon and knew Ernie.

They all literally grabbed me, stroked my arms, wiped tears from their eyes, and hustled me into the cottage where Ernie's father was born. I had planned to spend two hours in Rostin, which proved to be impossible. They sent out word somehow that I was there, and from 11 a.m. that day until noon the next, I saw cousins from four cities and a good number of Ernie's nieces, grand-nieces, nephews, and grand-nephews. Antonin's wife gave me a beautiful lace tablecloth she had made. I said I would take it to Ernie's family. She said, "No, it's for you. They get one when they come."

—PCV Czech Republic

II.3—SCORE YOURSELF— UNIVERSALIST OR PARTICULARIST ✍

Having become familiar with the two poles of this concept in the previous exercise, you now have a chance to think of your own behavior in the context of this important cultural dimension. Before reading further, take a moment to decide whether you consider yourself more of a universalist or a particularist.

Below are a number of paired statements (a. and b.). Circle the one which best describes the action you would take or the way you feel about the particular topic. Please choose one or the other even if you think both are true. Try to be as honest as you can by answering quickly and without too much thinking.

1a.	In hiring someone, I want to know about their technical skills and their educational/professional background.	**1b.**	In hiring, I want to know who the person's family and friends are, who will vouch for this person.
2a.	In society, we should help those who are the neediest.	**2b.**	In society, we should help the neediest of those who depend on us.
3a.	There are no absolutes in life; you always have to look at the particular situation.	**3b.**	There are certain absolutes which apply across the board.
4a.	I would be very hurt if my neighbor, a policeman, gave me a ticket for speeding.	**4b.**	I would not expect my neighbor, the policeman, to jeopardize his job and not give me a speeding ticket.
5a.	The courts should mediate conflicts.	**5b.**	People should solve their own conflicts; it's embarrassing if it has to go to court.
6a.	In general, people can be trusted.	**6b.**	My closest associates can be trusted absolutely; everyone else is automatically suspect.

—INSIGHT—

The relationship between individual and social ethics is influenced by culture.

7a. Performance reviews should not take personal relations into account.

7b. Performance reviews inevitably take personal relations into account.

8a. You often have to make exceptions for people because of circumstances.

8b. Exceptions should be very rare; otherwise, you open the floodgates,

9a. Contracts aren't necessary between friends.

9b. Contracts guarantee that friends stay friends.

10a. What is ethical in a given situation depends on who you are dealing with.

10b. Ethics are ethics no matter who you are dealing with.

Now that you have made your selections, turn to page 239 for results, and then calculate whether you came out more on the universalist or particularist side. Is your score here consistent with your self-concept?

II.4—THINKING IT THROUGH ✑

Look again at the statements in the preceding exercise and at the characteristics in the exercise before that. Can you see any examples or "proof" of universalist or particularist tendencies in your host culture?

Are there features of each approach that you like or agree with? What?

Are there features of each approach you don't like or disagree with? What?

CHAPTER THREE ✎
STYLES OF COMMUNICATION

Communication, the sending and receiving of messages, is an integral part of culture. Edward Hall, the noted interculturalist, has maintained that culture *is* communication. What he probably means is that since culture is such an important ingredient in all behavior, and so much of behavior is spent in one type of communicating or another, then it's hard to tell where one ends and the other takes over. In any event, whether or not they are one and the same, culture and communication certainly go hand in hand.

In the cross-cultural context, communication, like everything else, is more complicated. It's almost impossible to send a message that does not have at least some cultural content, whether it's in the words themselves, in the way they are said, or in the nonverbal signals that accompany them. And even if it were possible to *send* a message without any cultural content, it's not possible to receive one without passing it through the filter of one's own cultural conditioning. All of which means that host country people may not interpret everything you say the way you meant it. And vice versa.

Communication problems, especially misunderstanding and misinterpretation, are one of the most common frustrations experienced by PCVs. In this chapter, you will examine your own style of communication and then compare it to that of the host country, a process which should highlight some of the likelier challenges that await you.

Every country has its own way of saying things. The important thing is that which lies behind people's words.

—Freya Stark,
The Journey's Echo

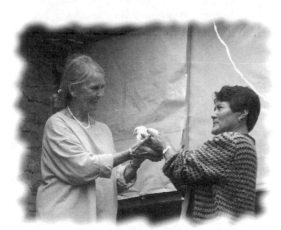

3.1—DEAR GAVIN ✍

Jan has finished training now and settled in at her site. In this letter to her PCV friend Gavin, Jan recounts the experience she recently had negotiating her living arrangements. As she relates the encounter with her landlord, she describes at least five common techniques of indirect communication. See if you can find them.

The immature rice stalk stands erect, while the mature stalk, heavy with grain, bends over.

—Cambodian proverb

Dear Gavin:

1. How are things out east? I've heard so much about your part of the country I've decided I will have to come and see for myself, maybe in the new year. Will you be around in January?

2. Settling in has been the circus I was more or less expecting. Some parts of it have gone quite smoothly; other parts haven't even begun to resolve themselves yet. By far the most intriguing aspect of settling in was trying to rent a room. I had this most amazing conversation with my landlord; it was the kind of cross-cultural incident they told us about in training, where you go along thinking one thing is happening and the other person is thinking something entirely different.

3. Anyway, I found a room I liked in a nice enough house and met with the landlord to discuss terms and price. One issue we had to resolve was whether I could use the attic to store some of my things, as my room had no extra space at all. I asked if it would be OK, and he said "Yes. If you like." Then he launched into a story, whose point I never did grasp, about how in his culture the aim in life is to be able to see the folly of attachments and to divest ourselves of material possessions as we get older, that these things blind us to the more important truths that we should be looking for if we're ever going to understand the meaning of life. I'm sure he's right, but I just wanted to rent a room.

4. Then we moved on to the problem of my meals and whether or not I could eat with the family, or if I should make other arrangements. By way of "response," he started talking

(continued)

about how close his house was to my work, which would be very convenient for me, so we still haven't resolved the meals question yet.

5. Next, it was time to talk about price. When I asked him how much he would charge, he blushed and said he had no idea. "Why don't you suggest a price?" he asked. I know what the going rate is in this town, so I told him 200. "That's good," he said. "Don't you think?" I said I thought it was fine, and asked him whether or not I needed to sign something, and when I might be able to move in. He said it was not necessary to sign a contract, and then asked me if I was sure I was happy with the price. I assured him I was.

6. He looked taken aback, and then asked me if I thought the room had enough space for all my possessions. "Americans have so many nice and useful things," he said. I said that so long as I could store some things in his attic, as he had promised, I would be fine. "Ah, yes," he said. "My attic. My poor, little attic. And all your wonderful things. And so little money you are paying me."

And there we were: back to square one.

It's much more fun in the retelling, I can assure you, but it all ended well, nearly an hour later, when we came to terms and finally understood each other.

I meant to write more, but my candle is low, (the power is out again) and dawn comes early here. All the best, and write me back immediately.

Jan

3.2—STYLES OF COMMUNICATION— INDIRECT AND DIRECT

Interculturalists have identified numerous differences in communication styles from culture to culture. The most important and most studied distinctions are the indirect/direct, or high context/low context, dichotomy described below:

Indirect/High Context—

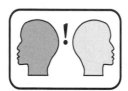

Context refers to the amount of innate and largely unconscious understanding a person can be expected to bring to a particular communication setting. In high context cultures, such as Thailand, which tend to be homogenous and collectivist, people carry within them highly developed and refined notions of how most interactions will unfold, of how they and the other person will behave in a particular situation. Because people in high context cultures already know and understand each other quite well, they have evolved a more indirect style of communication. They have less need to be explicit and rely less on words to convey meaning—and especially on the *literal* meaning of the spoken word— and more on nonverbal communication. People often convey meaning or send messages by manipulating the context. Because these cultures tend to be collectivist, people work closely together and know what everyone else knows. The overriding goal of the communication exchange is maintaining harmony and saving face.

Direct/Low Context—

Low context cultures, like the United States, tend to be more heterogeneous and individualist and accordingly have evolved a more direct communication style. Less can be assumed about the other person in a heterogeneous society, and less is known about others in a culture where people prefer independence, self-reliance, and a greater emotional distance from each other. They cannot depend merely on manipulating context—*not* doing or *not* saying something that is always done or said in that situation—or communicating nonverbally to make themselves understood; they must rely more on words, and on those words being interpreted *literally*. Getting or giving information is the goal of most communication exchanges.

The exercise below helps you define the differences. In the underlined space before each of the numbered statements, write "I" if you think it applies to a culture where communication is indirect/high context, or "D" if communication is direct/low context.

CHARACTERISTICS & BEHAVIORS

1. ____ Communication is like that between twins.

2. ____ People are reluctant to say no.

3. ____ You have to read between the lines.

4. ____ Use of intermediaries or third parties is frequent.

5. ____ Use of understatement is frequent.

6. ____ It's best to tell it like it is.

7. ____ It's okay to disagree with your boss at a meeting.

8. ____ "Yes" means yes.

9. ____ "Yes" means I hear you.

10. ____ Communication is like that between two casual acquaintances.

11. ____ It's not necessary to read between the lines.

12. ____ People engage in small talk and catching up before getting down to business.

13. ____ Business first, then small talk.

14. ____ Lukewarm tea means all is not well.

15. ____ Lukewarm tea means the tea got cold.

16. ____ People need to be brought up to date at a meeting.

17 ____ People are already up to date.

18. ____ The rank/status of the messenger is as important as the message.

19. ____ The message is what counts, not who the messenger is.

20. ____ People tell you what they think you want to hear.

—INSIGHT—

Different styles of communication mean an increased possibility of misunderstanding and misinterpretation.

[For suggested answers, see page 239.]

It would be a social insult for a <u>campesino</u> to tell a <u>gringo</u> that he's not going to come to a meeting. He says "yes," and so the meeting is scheduled. Twenty-five people said they'd come and two show up, and those two are not among the twenty-five who said they'd come.

—Peace Corps staff member

3.3—CLASH OF STYLES? ✍

The American style of communication, which is more direct than that of many other cultures, can affect your relations with host country nationals. Can you think of any times thus far in country when, in retrospect, you might have come on too strong, been too blunt, blurted out what was on your mind, or otherwise disturbed the harmony of a situation, or caused someone to lose face? Can you, alternatively, think of any examples of host country communication which, in retrospect, might have meant other than what you took them to mean? Note such incidents in the space below:

3.4—CULTURE & COMMUNICATION STYLES—AMERICAN AND HOST COUNTRY VIEWS COMPARED ✍

This exercise asks you to examine American, host country, and your own communication style in the context of direct vs. indirect styles. The mechanism used here is a continuum: a line with opposite views or positions presented at each end.

Four communication topics are listed, with a continuum for each. Put the letters "U.S." on that point on the line that you think best represents the "typical American" view of that topic; then, after consulting with a host country informant or a knowledgeable PCV, mark each continuum with the letters "H.C." to indicate the typical host country position.

STYLES OF COMMUNICATION—CONTINUUM

Degree of Directness

Direct   Indirect

←――――――――――――――――――――――――――――――――――→

People say what they mean and mean what they say; you don't need to read between the lines; it's important to tell it like it is; honesty is the best policy; the truth is more important than sparing someone's feelings.

People are indirect; they imply / suggest what they mean; understatement is valued; you need to read between the lines; the truth, if it hurts, should be tempered.

The Role of Context

Low Context   High Context

←――――――――――――――――――――――――――――――――――→

Low context, heterogenous and individualist cultures: little is already known; the message must be explicit and spelled out; words are the primary means of communication; nonverbal cues are not the key to understanding.

High context, homogenous and collectivist cultures: much is already known; the spoken word is not the primary means of communicating; much is implied but little needs to be said; nonverbal cues and the context are the key what is <u>not</u> said may be the message.

The Importance of Face

Face Less Important   Face Is Key

Face has moderate importance; the facts and expediency are more important than being careful about what you say; getting/ giving information is the overriding goal of the communication exchange; criticism is straightforward; it's okay to say no, to confront people.

Face is paramount; saving face/ not losing face takes precedence over the "truth"; maintaining harmony is the overriding goal of the communication exchange; confrontation is avoided; saying no is difficult; criticism is handled very delicately; what one says and what one feels often are not the same.

The Task or The Person

The Task   The Person

The task is separated from the person; do business first and then have small talk; establishing rapport/good personal relationship is not essential to getting the job done. The goal is accomplishing the task.

The task and the person can't be separated; begin with small talk and then move to business; personal relationship is a prerequisite to getting the job done. The goal is building the relationship.

CONTINUUM NOTES

In the space below, note any continuum in which the U.S. and H.C. marks are at opposite ends, and then indicate specifically how you think host country nationals would perceive your behavior in this respect. Using the Task or Person continuum, for example, you might observe that "They think I'm too work oriented or too impersonal."

Continuum: _____

How HCNs perceive me as an American:

Continuum: _____

How HCNs perceive me as an American:

—INSIGHT—

Americans and host country nationals have different views on fundamental aspects of communication.

Remember that where a culture's mark is on the continuum represents what the people in that country think of as normal, natural, right, or good, and that it is from this perspective that they will be judging and interpreting the behavior of others.

[When you have finished, turn to page 240 for possible perceptions.]

Observation Activity

3.5—NONVERBAL COMMUNICATION— GESTURES, EYE CONTACT & CONVERSATIONAL STYLE ꝏ

Communication falls into two classic categories: verbal and nonverbal. Nonverbal communication, in turn, can be divided into a number of specific subcategories. Two separate exercises (3.5 & 3.7) will be presented, each focusing on three types of nonverbal communication. These exercises may be completed over time, as you continue to become aware of personal, familial, and work behaviors in your host country.

GESTURES

In a number of different settings, watch what people do with their arms, hands, fingers, and whole body. Try to describe the gestures as "scientifically" as possible (a man held out his hand, palm down, and wiggled his fingers to call a waiter to his table) and indicate what you think is the meaning.

Hands	Arms
Fingers	**Whole Body**

EYE CONTACT

Observe the degree and nature of eye contact in as many of the following situations as possible:

Between two men of the same age	Between two women of the same age
Between an older and younger man/woman	Between a man and woman
Between a husband and wife in public	Between a boss and employee
Between a teacher and a student	Between a parent and child
Between people passing on the street	

Some social situations require body contact between members of the same sex. This entails being held by the elbow, kissing on both cheeks, being kissed on the hand, talking at unnaturally close range, or occasionally holding little fingers.

—PCV Afghanistan

1. In situations where host country people maintain _more_ eye contact than Americans normally do, how might Americans come across to host country nationals?

2. How might host country people come across to Americans in those same situations?

—INSIGHT—

The meaning of gestures, eye contact, and conversational patterns may not be the same in the host culture as in American culture.

3. In situations where host country people maintain _less_ eye contact than Americans usually do, how might Americans come across?

4. How might host country people come across to Americans in those same situations?

CONVERSATIONAL STYLE

Observe the following nonverbal aspects of typical conversations:

1. How much gesturing goes on in general?

2. How does the transition from one speaker to the next take place? Check one:

_____ speaker A starts before speaker B finishes

_____ speaker A starts just after speaker B finishes

_____ speaker A pauses before starting

3. How long does one person speak before allowing the other to speak?

4. How do people indicate they want to end the conversation?

5. How do people show disagreement?

6. How do people show displeasure with what they hear?

7. How do people show pleasure at what they are hearing?

8. What is the pattern of eye contact between speaker and listener?

3.6—DIALOGUES ✍

Each of the dialogues presented here contains an example of a misunderstanding due to differences in communication styles—indirect in one culture, direct in the other. Your task is to note in the space below each dialogue the *difference* between what was said or done and how the PCV interpreted it.

QUICK TRIP

HCN: How did the visit to the co-op go?

PCV: Quite well, I think they're interested in using my expertise.

HCN: Did they show you around?

PCV: Yes. I saw the whole co-op.

HCN: The whole thing! That must have taken hours.

PCV: Actually, we were in and out in less than 30 minutes. They said another guy was coming at noon.

COMMITTEE MEETING

1st PCV: How did it go with the committee members?

2nd PCV: A lot easier than I was expecting.

1st PCV: Really? Did you ask about buying the new equipment?

2nd PCV: Yes. I explained we had to have it and told them how much it would cost.

1st PCV: And?

2nd PCV: There was no discussion. They said fine and asked me to move on to the next item.

WE'LL GET BACK TO YOU

HCN: How did it go at the clinic?

PCV: Very well, I think, for the first meeting.

HCN: When will you see the director again?

PCV: In the end, I didn't meet with the director. I met with his assistant.

HCN: Did she ask you a lot of questions about your proposal?

PCV: A few.

HCN: When are you going back?

PCV: Probably next week.

HCN: You're not sure?

PCV: I asked for another appointment and she said she would get back to me.

EXPLANATIONS*

PCV: Miss Chung. What can I do for you?

HCN: Excuse me. I need some help with this new machine.

PCV: Of course. Let me explain it again.

HCN: I asked Li, but she couldn't help me.

PCV: No, she hasn't tried it yet.

HCN: It's a little bit complicated.

PCV: It's very complicated, but after I explained it to you and asked you if you understood, you said yes.

HCN: Yes. Please excuse me.

*Craig Storti. _Cross-Cultural Dialogues_, reprinted with permission of Intercultural Press, Inc., Yarmouth, ME. Copyright, 1994.

TRANSFER

1st PCV: I asked the director for a transfer yesterday.

2nd PCV: What did she say?

1st PCV: Not much. She asked me how I was getting along with Radu these days.

2nd PCV: What did you say?

1st PCV: I told her nothing had changed, that I wanted out because of him.

2nd PCV: Then what?

1st PCV: She said she understood my problem, that she knows Radu isn't easy.

2nd PCV: Do you think she'll transfer you?

1st PCV: Oh, I'm sure. She said she'd had a lot of complaints about Radu over the years.

—INSIGHT—

In some cultures, the real message is between the lines.

[For notes on the dialogues, turn to page 240.]

Observation Activity

3.7—NONVERBAL COMMUNICATION— FACIAL EXPRESSIONS, PERSONAL SPACE & TOUCHING ✍

This is the second of two exercises in which you observe and record instances of nonverbal communication. In this activity, you focus on facial expressions, personal space, and touching:

FACIAL EXPRESSIONS

Observe what people do with their head, eyes, eyebrows, mouth, nose, chin, etc. Record these observations as accurately as you can in the spaces below, indicating what these facial expressions mean:

The Head and Forehead	Eyes and eyebrows
The Nose	The Chin and Jaw
Any part of the face or head in combination with the hands and fingers	

PERSONAL SPACE

Observe how close various kinds of people stand to each other in various settings:

In normal conversation, at work, or on the street	
In line at the post office, bank, cinema, etc.	
In an elevator, crowded or uncrowded	
Two men	Two women
Two children	An older and younger person
Parent and child	A man and woman
Husband and wife	HCN and PCV

1. In those situations where host country people stand <u>closer</u> to each other than do Americans, what impression might people have of Americans?

—INSIGHT—

Interpret facial expressions from the host country culture's point of view, not your own.

2. What impression might Americans have of host country people in those same situations?

3. In those situations where host country people stand <u>further apart</u> from each other than do Americans, what impression might people have of Americans?

4. What impression might Americans have of host country people in those same situations?

TOUCHING

Observe how much and in which parts of the body the following people touch each other:

Two men	Two women
Husband and wife	Unrelated man and woman
Parent and child	Older and younger person
Boss and subordinate	Male boss/female worker and vice versa

What differences do you observe in touching behavior in public and in private?

1. In those situations where host country people touch each other _more_ than Americans do, what impression might people have of Americans?

2. What impression might host country people convey in those same situations?

3. In those situations where host country people touch _less_ than Americans do, what impression might people have of Americans?

4. What might be the impression of host country people?

3.8—PRACTICING INDIRECTNESS ✍

The next two exercises give you a chance to practice the skill of indirect communication. In this first activity, you are presented with a series of seven direct statements. Try to rephrase them to make them more indirect, writing your suggestions in the blank space below each one. While these statements could be appropriate in some situations, the setting here is a meeting, where allowing people to save face is important. Suggested rephrasing of the first statement is offered as an example.

It's just not in their culture to tell or even suggest what they think you should do. Even when you are asking for advice, I don't think they feel comfortable giving it. The direct American style is often taken as impolite.

—PCV Papua New Guniea

—INSIGHT—

The direct way of saying certain things may strike some listeners as too harsh.

1.	I don't think that's such a good idea.	*Do you think that's a good idea?* *Are there any other ideas?* *I like most parts of that idea.*
2.	That's not the point.	
3.	I think we should....	
4.	What do you think, Mr. Cato? *(Calling on people sometimes embarrasses them. How can you find out what Mr. Cato thinks without directly asking him?)*	
5.	Those figures are not accurate.	
6.	You're doing that wrong.	
7.	I don't agree.	

[See page 241 for suggestions.]

3.9—DECODING INDIRECTNESS ‿

This exercise is the opposite of the one you just completed. In this activity, you are presented with a series of indirect statements and asked to decode them—to explain in direct language what the speaker probably means. Looking at the first statement, "That is a very interesting viewpoint," remember that the person may mean exactly that, but *sometimes* it's an indirect way of saying "I disagree with you." In communicating across cultures, you need to *at least entertain the possibility* that the speaker may mean something other than what he or she has said. The first statement has been rephrased for you.

1.	That is a very interesting viewpoint.	*I don't agree.* *We need to talk more about this.* *You're wrong.*
2.	This proposal deserves further consideration.	
3.	I know very little about this, but....	
4.	We understand your proposal very well.	
5.	We will try our best.	
6.	I heard another story about that project.	
7.	Can we move on to the next topic?	

[See page 242 for suggestions.]

—INSIGHT—

The actual meaning of the words may be a poor guide to what an indirect communicator is saying.

NEIGHBORS

Coming from brash America, we have to look hard to pick out the subtle feedback we don't even realize we're being given.

—PCV Fiji

I spent most of the afternoon writing letters, catching up on correspondence that had piled up in my mailbox while I was away. I was also conveniently avoiding the heat and, to some degree, the village itself. At the moment, it didn't feel like the place where I wanted to be.

A cool breeze from the mountains picked up late in the afternoon. I took advantage of the cooler air to get a little exercise and walked to the post office. When I started back, the rain was looking like a sure thing. Little dust devils were whirling around in the dirt streets, and withered leaves twirled down from the sycamore trees that formed an arcade over the wide, dilapidated street. Dark clouds were bearing down from the mountains to the south. I picked up my pace.

Down the street, coming towards me, was a woman wrapped up in a turquoise *jellaba*. I recognized her as my downstairs neighbor. As we continued towards each other, we were nearly jogging, trying to reach our destinations before the rain. We exchanged the minimum smiles and hello, how-are-yous as we passed.

"Please tell Aisha to put the goats in the shed, it's going to rain,." she shouted at me over her shoulders as she continued on her way.

"Okay," I said.

In that moment, I had such a feeling of elation! Why, over something so small and trivial? Because she said it in Arabic, not in French. Because she didn't slow it down or dress it up for speaking to a foreigner. Because she said it to me in the same way she would have said it to one of her own children or one of her other neighbors, without formality, without any awareness that she was talking to someone from the other side of the world, but just saying it the way she would normally say it. Because, after all, I was only her neighbor, no one strange or special. I was just the guy who lived upstairs.

—PCV Morocco

3.10—HARMONY AND SAVING FACE ✍

As noted earlier, indirect communication owes much to the importance many cultures place on preserving harmony and saving face. In this exercise, you are presented with a number of specific incidents that require diplomacy. Applying the skills and techniques you've learned in this chapter, write below each description how you would handle the situation to avoid causing embarrassment or loss of face.

CROP FAILURE

Your boss has come up with a new scheme for improving crop yields in your province. Since you are the technical expert in this area, he has come to ask you for your opinion. His scheme is based on unreliable data and will in all likelihood not work in your part of the country. It's possible farmers could lose their whole crop if they try this experiment. What is your response?

END RUN

In the clinic where you work, the supervisor you report to is ineffective. Because of this person's incompetence, the project you're working on is getting nowhere. You know if you could go directly to this person's superior, the manager of the entire division, you would get much better results—and get them much faster. But if you ignore or go around your supervisor, she will be hurt and embarrassed. How do you resolve this situation?

MOVING UP

The counterpart you work with is an agreable person but not very competent. Now your boss, who is also his boss, has called you into her office to ask you whether your counterpart should be promoted to a new position. How do you respond?

People tell you what they think you want to hear, which may not be what you need to know.

—PCV Fiji

ELECTRONIC MAIL

Three companies have been asked to bid the job of supplying electronic mail service to the organization you work for as a computer specialist. The ultimate decision will be made by your boss, but he is relying heavily on your advice in this matter. As it happens, a cousin of your boss owns one of these companies, the company asking for the most money and the least able to deliver the goods. Your boss asks you what you think of that company. What do you say?

TIGHT SPOT

At a faculty meeting, the head of your department states a position on an important matter. The school headmaster then turns to you and asks your opinion. You don't agree with the head of your department. Now what?

[For brief notes on these incidents, see page 242.]

DEAR GAVIN—AN ANALYSIS 🐉

Now that you have finished this chapter, read the letter to Gavin again and see if you can find some of the techniques of indirect communication discussed in these pages; then read the analysis below.

Paragraph 3—When the landlord says "Yes. If you like" to Jan's inquiry about using the attic, he is probably saying no. Yes, as you have seen, means little in some cultures, and a qualified yes (if you like) is even more problematic. The landlord next launches into a story about the advantages of owning little, which may be his polite way of saying that he won't be able to store Jan's many possessions in his attic. This fact becomes abundantly clear when we get to paragraph 6.

Paragraph 4—Indirect communicators often change the subject rather than disagree with or say no to someone, which may be why the landlord answers Jan's question about meals with a comeback about the convenient location of the house.

Paragraph 5—The landlord's reply to Jan's offer of 200, "That's good, don't you think?" is mere politeness. If he were pleased with 200, he would probably have been much more positive. Any doubt is erased when he then asks her if she thinks 200 is enough; if he thought it was enough, he wouldn't have asked. She interprets his question as a real question, when it is in fact a way of expressing disagreement or disapproval. When he then goes back to the matter, asking her if she's happy with the price, he is signaling that *he* is not happy with it, but she still doesn't understand.

Paragraph 6—Now we get the answer to the inquiry about using the attic. Since she thought he gave permission (Yes. If you like) but he did not, he has to come back to the matter to clarify it. He's not going to say no, but he gives enough hints, and then brings up the price again.

To summarize, these are techniques of indirect communication illustrated here:

1. Using a qualifed yes to mean no.
2. Telling a story as a way of saying no delicately.
3. Changing the subject to avoid saying no.
4. Asking a question to give a negative answer.
5. Returning to a previous point of discussion to signal disagreement.

Khoo Ah Au liked Americans. Above all he found their personal relationships easy to read. His own people were always very careful not to give themselves away, to expose crude feelings about one another. Americans seemed not to care how much was understood by strangers. It was almost as if they enjoyed being transparent.

—*Eric Ambler,*
Passage of Arms

JOURNAL ENTRY 3

What have you learned about your communication style in this chapter? Are you going to have to make adjustments in your style? Do you think you normally interpret the remarks of host country people correctly? How can you be yourself, yet still respect host country norms of preserving harmony and saving face?

FUNDAMENTALS OF CULTURE III
THE CONCEPT OF TIME ✖

This exercise introduces the third of the four fundamentals of culture: the concept of time. The two poles of this dimension, monochronic and polychronic, are defined and explored in the activity immediately following this one.

III.1—SERVICE WITH A SMILE ✖

The drawing below represents a shopkeeper standing behind the counter in his shop. Imagine six patrons ready to check out. Using circles to represent them, draw a diagram of how the patrons should arrange themselves in front of the counter.

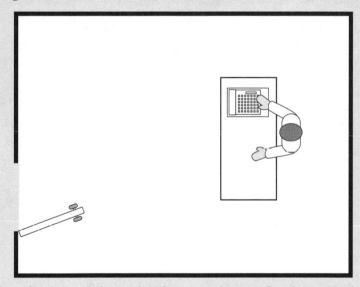

On what basis did you decide to put the people where you did?

The post office offered the usual experience: a cluster of people mashed together in front of the sullen clerk, all thrusting their business in his face, with a line of the less determined off to one side, standing patiently in the belief they would be waited on sometime.

—PCV Morocco

—INSIGHT—

Lining up and not lining up are culturally determined behaviors.

[For a drawing of how people from a different culture would stand in this situation, see page 243.]

III.2—CONCEPT OF TIME— MONOCHRONIC AND POLYCHRONIC

Another of the ways in which cultures differ is in how people conceive of and handle time, and how their concept of time affects their interactions with each other. In this activity, you are given a general description of the two poles or extremes of this dimension—monochronic and polychronic*—and then asked to assign characteristics to one category or the other. The two poles are described below:

Monochronic—

Time is the given and people are the variable. The needs of people are adjusted to suit the demands of time—schedules, deadlines, etc. Time is quantifiable, and a limited amount of it is available . People do one thing at a time and finish it before starting something else, regardless of circumstances.

Polychronic—

Time is the servant and tool of people. Time is adjusted to suit the needs of people. More time is always available, and you are never too busy. People often have to do several things simultaneously, as required by circumstances. It's not necessary to finish one thing before starting another, nor to finish your business with one person before starting in with another.

*Based on concepts developed by Edward T. Hall, <u>The Silent Language</u>, 1959 and <u>The Dance of Life</u>, Anchor-Doubleday, 1983.

In the underlined blank space before each of the behaviors or characteristics listed below, put "M" if you think it is *more likely* to apply to a culture where time is monochronic and "P" if it is polychronic.

CHARACTERISTICS & BEHAVIORS

—INSIGHT—

Time is a cultural phenomenon.

1. ____ Time is money.

2. ____ To be late is rude.

3. ____ Schedules are sacred.

4. ____ The focus is on the task, getting the job done.

5. ____ Being made to wait is normal.

6. ____ Interruptions are life.

7. ____ Plans are fixed, once agreed upon.

8. ____ This attitude is consistent with an individualist viewpoint.

9. ____ The focus is on the person, establishing a relationship

10. ____ This attitude is consistent with a collectivist viewpoint.

11. ____ Deadlines are an approximation.

12. ____ To be late is to be late.

13. ____ Focus on the internal clock.

14. ____ Plans are always changing.

15. ____ Having to wait is an insult.

16. ____ People are never too busy.

17. ____ Interruptions are bad.

18. ____ People stand in line.

[The answers appear on page 243.]

TIME TRIALS

Time always seems to be on their side.

—PCV Cameroon

At my site, I'm a 40-minute walk from the closest village where I do my shopping. Many of the stores are run out of villagers' homes, and these stores have taught me a lesson about Fiji. An Australian man once visited the island while doing research and asked me when the stores were open, since it was afternoon and he hadn't seen an open store yet. Taken aback by what seemed at the time an incredibly stupid question, I told him the obvious truth. "They're open when their doors are open." It was only when I walked away that I realized that it really wasn't such a stupid question and was a question I might have asked myself when I first arrived on Fiji. Having lived on Lakeba for a year at that time, I had learned my lesson and knew that time is a foreign concept. The stores were open when the villagers decided they had something to sell. Some days they're open; some days they're not.

When I first traveled out to my island via the cargo ship, I was told to report at 4:00 p.m. Tuesday. We left late in the day on Thursday. Welcome to a tiny island in the South Pacific.

—PCV Fiji

III.3—SCORE YOURSELF— MONOCHRONIC & POLYCHRONIC

The exercise below can help you to discover whether your own concept of time is more monochronic or polychronic. After reading the paired statements (a. and b.), circle the one that best describes the action you would take or the way you feel about the particular topic.

1a. People should stand in line so they can be waited on one at a time.

1b. There's no need to stand in line, as people will be waited on as they are ready for service.

2a. Interruptions usually cannot be avoided and are often quite beneficial.

2b. Interruptions should be avoided wherever possible.

3a. It's more efficient if you do one thing at a time.

3b. I can get as much done if I work on two or three things at the same time.

4a. It's more important to complete the transaction.

4b. It's more important to stick to the schedule.

5a. Unanticipated events are hard to accommodate and should be avoided where possible.

5b. Unexpected things happen all the time; that's life.

6a. You shouldn't take a telephone call or acknowledge a visitor when you are meeting with another person.

6b. It would be rude not to take a phone call if I'm in, or to ignore a visitor who drops by.

7a. You shouldn't take deadlines too seriously; anything can happen. What's a deadline between friends?

7b. Deadlines are like a promise; many other things depend on them, so they should not be treated lightly.

8a. It's important, in a meeting or a conversation, not to become distracted or digress. You should stick to the agenda.

8b. Digressions, distractions are inevitable. An agenda is just a piece of paper.

9a. I tend to be people-oriented.

9b. I tend to be task-oriented.

10a. Personal talk is part of the job.

10b. Personal talk should be saved for after hours or during lunch.

—INSIGHT—

Time means different things
in different cultures.

Now that you have made your selections, turn to page 244 for results, and then calculate whether you came out more on the monochronic or polychronic side. Is your score here consistent with your self-concept?

Keep in mind that there is nothing scientific about this exercise, that it doesn't prove anything about you. After all, most of the paired statements are taken out of context; you might select one alternative in one set of circumstances and the opposite in another set. Even so, you have at least been exposed to some alternative behaviors and ways of thinking and perhaps been given some food for thought.

III.4—INDICATIONS ◦

By now you must have encountered examples of either monochronic or polychronic behaviors in your host country, though you may not have known what to call them. What examples have you noticed? The next time you're in a public place, notice whether people line up. Try to notice whether people interrupt other people in "private" conversation more or less than in the U.S.

Are there aspects of each approach that you like and agree with? What?

Are there aspects of each approach you dislike and disagree with? What?

In urban America, five minutes is the basic unit of meaningful time. Turkish time is built on considerably longer meaningful units. Waiting thirty to sixty minutes for a well-placed official is normal. Highly valued time is, after all, a byproduct of industrial society.

—*PCV Turkey*

CHAPTER FOUR ✐
CULTURE IN THE WORKPLACE

Culture comes into its own in human interactions, and one of the greatest arenas for such interaction is the place where people work. In preceding chapters, you considered how culture would affect you on the job. Here, you examine the impact of culture on a variety of work-related norms and behaviors, paying particular attention to three dimensions of cultural difference that have special implications for the workplace:

1. the concept of power and power distance;

2. attitudes toward uncertainty and the unknown; and

3. the concept of status.

The first month or two in class I was always saying, "Look at me when I talk to you," and the kids simply wouldn't do it. They would always look at their hands, or the blackboard, or anywhere except looking me in the face. And finally one of the other teachers told me it was a cultural thing. They should warn us about things like that.

—Tony Hillerman
Skinwalkers

4.1—FROM JAN'S JOURNAL ✍

Jan has now been at her site a little over a year. In this excerpt from her journal, she writes about her experiences at the local AIDS clinic where she volunteers one day a week. Her task there is to work with a local health educator and design posters and illustrated pamphlets to use in AIDS education talks at the clinic and in nearby villages. In her interactions with clinic employees, she has run into a number of workplace issues. As you read her journal, mark where you think Jan misunderstood workplace norms, or projected some of her own attitudes and values onto the host culture.

September 21

1. *The saga continues at the clinic. I think I understand better how things work around here, but I have to say I'm not happy with my progress, or lack of progress. I've made some very good friends, one or two of whom even confide in me, but I didn't come to this country just to make friends. The problem seems to be a lack of funds to buy the materials I need to get started.*

2. *Actually, that's not 100 percent true; the money is there, but it's not coming to me. I've asked several times, but everyone says it's up to Mr. Beton, the clinic manager, with whom I've never even had a one-on-one meeting. I did meet him in the beginning, when I first came here, but he was with a lot of other people, so I didn't get to discuss my project. I did meet his boss one afternoon, though, when she was on a tour of the clinic and passed by my office. She asked me how things were going, and I said fine, except I had no money to buy materials. She said she would check into it, but nothing has happened. A few days after that, I asked for a meeting with Mr. Beton, but so far, he hasn't responded.*

3. *While I'm waiting for some movement, I've stumbled across another job I can do. I noticed one day that the clinic has no sign-in forms to record the number of visitors each day. I know the clinic needs this information because the ministry asks for these numbers every quarter, and the clinic's annual budget allocation is*

(continued)

based in part on this information. The clinic used to have a form, someone told me, but ran out of copies several months ago, so the receptionist just keeps track with tick marks on a piece of paper. I asked what the old form looked like and then designed a new one and showed it to the man in charge of volunteers. He said it was nice and took it away for approval. I expect it will show up any day now at the front desk.

*   **4.** *I guess the lesson in all this is that you have to make your own work, not wait around to be told what to do (like most of the staff here seems to do). Once you start looking for ways you can make yourself useful, there's no end to what you can do. At a staff meeting they invited me to the other day, I explained about the new sign-in form and asked people in other departments to let me know if they had similar things I could do for them. I then mentioned again that since I wasn't getting the money I needed for my primary project, I had plenty of time to work on other things.*

*   **5.** *A funny thing happened at that same meeting. Mr. Beton wasn't there, so his deputy ran the meeting. One item on the agenda was a report on the progress of the addition that's being built on the back of the clinic, to consist of two more examining rooms and two waiting rooms. Ground was broken last month, but nothing—and I mean nothing—has happened since. But in his report, the deputy said we had made great progress on the addition. When I asked him when construction was going to start, he said he didn't know!*

*   **6.** *I try hard to take all this in stride. I know things take longer here, so I'm not ready to throw in the towel or anything, but I do think I've been here long enough now to establish my good faith and credibility.*

4.2—CONCEPT OF POWER— HIGH & LOW POWER DISTANCE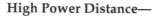

In this exercise, you consider the notion of power distance; a manifestation of the attitude of a society toward inequality—how cultures deal with people's different levels of status and their access to power. It is manifest especially in workplace relations, particularly in the role and relationship of the manager and the subordinate. The following brief descriptions of the two poles of this concept—high and low power distance*—suggest the issues involved:

High Power Distance—

People in these cultures accept that inequalities in power and status are natural or existential. In the same way they accept that some people are smarter than others, people accept that some will have more power and influence than others. Those with power tend to emphasize it, to hold it close and not delegate or share it, and to distinguish themselves as much as possible from those who do not have power. They are, however, expected to accept the responsibilities that go with power, to look after those beneath them. Subordinates are not expected to take initiative and are closely supervised.

Low Power Distance—

People in these cultures see inequalities in power and status as largely artificial; it is not natural, though it may be convenient, that some people have power over others. Those with power, therefore, tend to deemphasize it, to minimize the differences between themselves and subordinates, and to delegate and share power to the extent possible. Subordinates are rewarded for taking initiative and do not like close supervision.

Based on concepts developed by Geert Hofstede, <u>Culture's Consequences,</u> Sage Publications, CA, 1980; and <u>Culture and Organizations:Software of the Mind,</u> McGraw-Hill, NY, 1997.

In the underlined space before each of the statements below, put an "H" if you think it reflects an attitude of high power distance, or an "L" if low power distance is more likely:

CHARACTERISTICS & BEHAVIORS

1. _____ People are less likely to question the boss.

2. _____ Elitism is the norm.

3. _____ Students question teachers.

4. _____ Freedom of thought is encouraged.

5. _____ Those in power have special privileges.

6. _____ The chain of command is mainly for convenience.

7. _____ There are greater wage differences between managers and subordinates.

8. _____ Workers prefer precise instructions from superiors.

9. _____ Interaction between boss and subordinate is more informal.

10. _____ Subordinates and bosses are interdependent.

11. _____ Bosses are independent; subordinates are dependent.

12. _____ Freedom of thought could get you into trouble.

13. _____ It's okay to question the boss.

14. _____ Less social mobility is the norm.

15. _____ The chain of command is sacred.

16. _____ The pecking order is clearly established.

17. _____ Management style is authoritarian and paternalistic.

18. _____ Management style is consultative and democratic.

19. _____ Interaction between boss and subordinate is formal.

—INSIGHT—

Power must be exercised more openly in some cultures than in others.

(for suggested answers, see page 244.)

4.3—TRUST 🐾

"Slowly, through ceaseless struggle and effort, I learned to overcome the day-to-day barriers that had previously seemed like indomitable walls. I became an accepted part of my rural community and mastered Spanish. I learned the simple truism that trust must precede change, and focused on making friends with the hill farmers rather than on counting the number of trees that got planted. And, sure enough, the less I focused on the work, the more work seemed to get done."

—**PCV Guatemala**

What lessons did this PCV learn that might be helpful to you in your assignment?

Why does he say that trust must precede change?

4.4—DIALOGUES ✍

Each of the dialogues that appears below contains an example of a cultural misunderstanding. The PCV does not recognize power distinctions in the same way as people in the host country. As you read each dialogue, note in the margin the *difference* in interpretation that you detect.

BOSSES HAVE THEIR REASONS

PCV: What did the headmistress decide?

HCN: She said we should put our plan in motion now.

PCV: But it's not ready.

HCN: I know, but she must have her reasons.

PCV: I don't think she's thought it through.

HCN: Maybe not, but she's the boss.

PCV: I'm going to talk to her. I think I can change her mind.

> *With the best leaders, when the work is done the task is accomplished, the people will say, we have done this ourselves.*
>
> —*Lao Tsu, China, 700 B.C.*

A SURPRISE FOR THE CHIEF

PCV: I finally figured out how to solve our storage problems.

HCN: How?

PCV: We could clean out that shed by the parking lot. It's full of rotting crates that aren't good anymore.

HCN: That's a great idea. What did Mr. Plonc say?

PCV: The chief? I didn't tell him yet. I want to surprise him.

THE GOLDEN SPOON

HCN: Where do you want to have lunch?

PCV: How about the Golden Spoon?

HCN: Fine.

PCV: I'm going to invite the provincial representative, since he's visiting.

HCN: Mr. Kamini? He won't eat with us. He'll eat with the supervisors.

PCV: He might like to let his hair down with us commoners.

—INSIGHT—

Interaction between manager and subordinate is influenced by culture.

A LESSON

APCD: Did you talk with your department head?

PCV: Mr. Biswas? I thought about it, but he's hopeless.

APCD: I know. He was given that job as a favor.

PCV: I'm going to go straight to the dean.

APCD: Now there's somebody who gets results.

PCV: Maybe this will teach Biswas a lesson.

APCD: How do you mean?

PCV: If you don't do your job, people will go around you.

[Turn to page 245 for an analysis.]

CROSS-CULTURAL DIALOGUE

The PCV: Even as I entered the pastel pink building, I noticed a strange absence of noise, considering it was the first day of school. A few isolated students wearing white school jackets rambled through the dimly lit hallway. I looked out into the school yard and saw piles of old desk fragments, broken bricks, and tree fragments. They must be cleaning the school grounds, I thought.

The classroom where I was to teach was located a short walking distance behind the main building. I hopped on my bicycle and coasted right up to my door. Two students were sitting inside playing cards. I looked at the official enrollment number of 47 and asked earnestly, "Where are the other forty-five students?" The card players faltered a bit and then mumbled, "They'll come by and by." "Well, let's start without them," I suggested, with a disapproving stare at the cards.

Her Students: It was Tito and Mando who came and told us that a skinny, sickly white woman had jumped off her bicycle, run into our classroom, and tried to teach them English that morning. Tito and Mando weren't even in our class! They were just sitting there, waiting to use the soccer field, when she rushed in like the rains. They weren't sure what to say because she looked so strange. Her hair was all falling down, and she wore a dress that looked like an old faded bed covering that one might have bought from a Mauritanian vendor in the used clothing market. We knew no one would be at school yet—most students were still on the farms, finishing the harvest—[but] we decided we would go the next day to see what this new American teacher looked like.

—PCV West Africa

4.5—ATTITUDE TOWARD UNCERTAINTY & THE UNKNOWN— HIGH & LOW UNCERTAINTY AVOIDANCE ☙

As Americans, we think we can pretty much do whatever we set our minds to. In Romania, things operate more [cautiously]. There is a great fear of risk.

—PCV Romania

The second of the three dimensions of culture that particularly affects the workplace is how people respond to the inherent uncertainty of life. This uncertainty creates anxiety in all cultures, with characteristic responses— technology to control uncertainty in the natural world; laws, regulations, and procedures to control the uncertainty in human behavior; and religion to address the question of transcendental uncertainty.

While all societies feel threatened by uncertainty, some feel more threatened by it than others do. Depending on their attitudes, different cultures have devised different norms and systems for dealing with it. The two extremes, called high uncertainty avoidance and low uncertainty avoidance,* are described below:

High Uncertainty Avoidance—
Cultures characterized by high uncertainty avoidance feel especially anxious about the uncertainty in life and try to limit and control it as much as possible. They have more laws, regulations, policies, and procedures and a greater emphasis on obeying them. They also have a strong tendency toward conformity, hence predictability. People take comfort in structure, systems, and expertise—anything that can blunt or even neutralize the impact of the unexpected. The unknown is frightening.

Low Uncertainty Avoidance—
People in these cultures do not feel quite so threatened nor anxious about uncertainty, and therefore do not have such a strong need to limit or control it. They seek to legislate fewer areas of human interaction and tolerate differences better. They feel boxed in by too much structure or too many systems. They are curious rather than frightened by the unknown and are not uncomfortable leaving things to chance. Life is interesting but not especially daunting.

*Based on concepts developed by Geert Hofstede, Culture's Consequences, Sage Publications, CA; 1980 and Culture and Organizations:Software of the Mind, McGraw-Hill, NY, 1997.

As you read the statements that follow, put an "H" in the underlined space preceding those you think relate to high uncertainty avoidance and an "L" where you think low uncertainty avoidance applies.

CHARACTERISTICS & BEHAVIORS

1. ____ Punctuality is highly valued.

2. ____ People should keep emotions under control.

3. ____ Different is dangerous.

4. ____ People change jobs with more frequency.

5. ____ People expect more formality in interactions.

6. ____ People more readily accept dissent.

7. ____ Take things one day at a time.

8. ____ People should let their emotions out.

9. ____ The chain of command should never be bypassed.

10. ____ Conflict in organizations is natural, nothing to be afraid of.

11. ____ People believe less in common sense.

12. ____ Conflict in organizations should be eliminated.

13. ____ Differences are curious.

14. ____ People change jobs infrequently.

15. ____ A general sense of anxiety prevails.

16. ____ A general sense of well-being prevails.

17. ____ People accept authority more readily; authority is comforting.

18. ____ People accept authority less readily; authority is limiting.

19. ____ Rules should not be broken.

20. ____ Rules can be broken if it makes sense, for pragmatic reasons.

21. ____ Risks should be avoided.

22. ____ Risks are opportunities.

—INSIGHT—

Attitudes toward the unknown shape many human behaviors.

[Turn to page 246 for suggested answers.]

4.6—DIALOGUES ✐

In the following dialogues, see if you can recognize evidence of high or low uncertainty avoidance; note your findings in the margins.

ABOUT MANUEL

PCV: How did your meeting go with Manuel?

HCN: Not very well. He's still seething about being passed over for that promotion.

PCV: Has he talked to the chief?

HCN: The chief knows.

PCV: But Manuel should get it off his chest if it's bothering him.

The Yapese concepts of time, work, and plan are radically different from ours. Yapese time means an hour or two later; work is a mixture of performing the task and getting updated on everyone from the coconut wireless; plan is a general discussion of something to be done without the details, the doers, the tasks, or the timeline.

—PCV Micronesia

IN OVER HIS HEAD

PCV: I think the consultant from the Ministry of the Environment is in over his head.

HCN: The expert from the capital?

PCV: Yeah, him.

HCN: But he has a Ph.D. and studied in France.

PCV: He still has no idea about how you change behavior in rural communities. His grazing proposal will never work here.

HCN: I heard some grumbling, actually. Maybe you're right. What do you think he should do?

PCV: It's simple, really. He should just admit he's wrong and start over again.

REGULATIONS

PCV: We're getting nowhere with the textbook project.

HCN: I know. The teachers are getting frustrated.

PCV: It's all because of that regulation against using money from other budgets, even if they have a surplus.

HCN: We're stuck with it, I'm afraid.

PCV: We could just ignore it and say we didn't know any better.

BACKLOG

HCN: Did you hear? We won't be getting a new staff person after all.

PCV: I know. So much for getting rid of our backlog.

HCN: Well, we can resubmit the request next summer.

PCV: Actually, I've got a better idea. I've heard about some new accounting software that would make our workload a lot easier.

HCN: Has it been tried in organizations like ours?

PCV: In America. I don't know about here. We could probably get it free if we asked.

HCN: And then train everyone in it?

PCV: Right.

—INSIGHT—

Your attitudes towards laws, regulations, policies, and procedures and the degree to which people must obey them may not be the same as those in your host country.

[An analysis of these dialogues appears on page 247.]

4.7—NO LEGS ✎

"From the reports on file, it was obvious that we hadn't accomplished anything at all after ten years of Peace Corps running the community center in Sedhiou. We had a library with no books, a milk program with no milk, and a pre-school with no education taking place. As I looked around the region, other foreign aid programs were no better. There was an agricultural college with no students, no materials, and no instructors—of which the town officials were very proud! There was a Taiwanese agricultural mission to teach advanced farming methods, totally ignored by the farmers."

—*PCV Senegal*

Why do you think such projects don't get off the ground?

How would you approach a community project in order to get a different result?

4.8—THE SOURCE OF STATUS—
ACHIEVED OR ASCRIBED ◈

This is the last of the three workplace-related cultural dimensions presented in this chapter: how people come by their status, in their organizations, and in society in general. This concept is related to power distance in some respects and to the individualism/collectivism dichotomy in others. Certain features, however, are outside of those two dimensions and deserve attention in their own right. The two poles here are sometimes referred to as achieved and ascribed, and in other cases, as "doing" cultures and "being" cultures. They are briefly described below.

Achieved Status—

In these *doing* cultures, people are looked up to and respected because of their personal and especially their professional accomplishments. You get ahead into positions of power and influence by virtue of your achievements and performance. Your status is earned and not merely a function of birth, age, or seniority. You are hired based on your record of success, not on the basis of family background, connections, or the school you attended. People aren't particularly impressed with titles. Education is important, but not the mere fact of it; you have to have done something with your knowledge. Status is not automatic and can be forfeited if you stop achieving.

Ascribed Status—

In these *being* cultures, a certain amount of status is built into the person; it is automatic and therefore difficult to lose. You are looked up to because of the family and social class you are born into, because of your affiliations and membership in certain important groups, and, later, because of your age and seniority. The school you went to and the amount of education you received also confer status, whether or not you did well in school or have done anything with your education. Titles are important and should always be used. You are pressured to justify the power, respect and deference that you automatically enjoy. While you cannot lose your status completely, you can lose respect by not realizing your potential.

The following incidents have come about in part because of cultural differences involving status; in the space below each description, write what you would do in the particular situation.

UPSTANDING STUDENTS

You are a high school teacher in your country. When you enter the classroom, all your students automatically stand up until you give them the signal to sit. You are uncomfortable with this deferential behavior and tell your students they need not stand when you enter the room. After two weeks, the headmaster asks to speak with you. He informs you that the other teachers have heard that your students don't stand when you enter the room and the teachers are upset. They regard this behavior as a sign of disrespect, which they fear may spread to their classrooms. They worry, moreover, that you deliberately may be trying to blur the distinction between teacher and student. If students put themselves on the same level as teachers, chaos will result. What should you do about the teachers' reactions?

RESPECT

You are an urban planner working for the city government. Every morning a truck bearing city sanitation laborers stops at your house to give you a ride to work. Your boss, an engineer, and a second professional always sit up front in the cab, but you like to sit in the back and banter with the laborers. After a few days, your boss says you are confusing the workers with your informal behavior and warns you that you will soon lose their respect if you don't start acting like a professional. How do you respond?

How can she understand our culture? She has only seen the rains fall once.

—HCN Guineau-Bissau

IN THE MATTER OF MR. KODO

You're being asked to take sides in a faculty dispute. A few weeks ago a vacancy occurred in the department of the university where you teach. The two candidates for the position, both college graduates, were an older man (Mr. Kodo) who has been at this school for 15 years and a younger man with more up-to-date technical credentials, a superior educational background, and two years of experience on this faculty. From a technical standpoint, the younger man was a much stronger candidate and also a more dynamic teacher, and he was in fact selected for the position by the British expatriate who chairs this department.

Mr. Kodo and many of his (and your) colleagues were stunned by the decision, seeing it as a repudiation of his years of experience and dedication to this institution. Mr. Kodo is extremely embarrassed at being passed over and has not appeared on campus since the announcement was made. Now his colleagues are circulating a petition to the chairman to reconsider his decision and put Mr. Kodo into the job he deserves. They have asked you to sign the petition, already signed by all of them as well as scores of students, and to participate actively in this campaign. You in fact feel the right choice was made and are reluctant to get involved, but you are under increasing pressure to "do the right thing." What do you do?

CONSIDERING THE SOURCE

You are the technical expert at a provincial agricultural extension office. A delegation from the Minister's office is coming next week to discuss an important change in policy. You are the person who can make the most substantive contribution to this discussion, but you are not being invited to the meeting. Instead, your boss has been picking your brain for days and has asked you to write a report for him containing all the important points he should make. Finally, you ask him why he doesn't just bring you along to the meeting and let you speak directly to the delegation. He says you're too young to be taken seriously, and besides, you're a woman. Your arguments are too important, he says, and he doesn't want them to be discounted because of their source. How do you feel, and what's your response?

[For suggested ideas, turn to page 248.]

4.9—WORKPLACE VALUES AND NORMS—COMPARING AMERICAN AND HOST COUNTRY VIEWS ༄

In this exercise, you compare the American and host country positions on key dimensions of culture that affect the workplace, including those discussed in this chapter—power distance, uncertainty avoidance, and source of status—as well as several others. Once again, as in Chapter Three, the mechanism used here is a continuum on which you indicate (with the letters H.C. and U.S.) where you think the cultures of your host country and the United States fit.

WORKPLACE VALUES AND NORMS—CONTINUUM

Power Distance

Low Power Distance   High Power Distance

◄─────────────────────────────►

Less distance, more interaction exists between the boss and subordinates. The boss is more democratic, delegates responsibility. Taking initiative is okay. It's also okay to disagree with or question the boss. The boss sees himself/herself as one of the group. Power is decentralized.

Greater distance exists between the boss and subordinates. Power is centralized and generally not shared. The boss does not delegate responsibilty or reward initiative. The worker does not disagree with or question the boss. The boss sees himself/herself as on one level, workers on another. The boss is more autocratic and paternalistic.

Uncertainty Avoidance

Low Uncertainty Avoidance   High Uncertainty Avoidance

◄─────────────────────────────►

The unknown need not be scary. Fewer laws exist and less emphasis is on conformity. It's okay to break laws for pragmatic reasons; it's okay to bypass the chain of command if necessary. Conflict can't always be avoided. Taking risks is acceptable. Interactions are more informal. Different is interesting.

The unknown must be controlled. More laws exist and greater emphasis is on obeying laws and conforming. It's never good to break laws or bypass the chain of command, whatever the reason. Conflict must be avoided; risks are not attractive. Interactions are more formal. Different is dangerous.

Source of Status

Achieved Status   Ascribed Status

←————————————————————————————→

Meritocracy exists. Status is earned by your achievements, by what you've accomplished in life. You get ahead based on merit. Status must be won, not automatically accorded, and it can be lost.

An autocracy exists. A certain amount of status comes with the family name and the groups you are affiliated with, and can't easily be lost. Achievements are important, but you can have status even without them. Your station in life is in part an accident of birth.

Concept of Work

Work As Part Of Identity   Work As Functional Necessity

←————————————————————————————→

Work has value in and of itself. Your job is an important part of your identity. People live to work, in the sense that getting things done is inherently satisfying.

Work is the means to paying bills and meeting financial obligations. It may be satisfying but doesn't have to be. Life is too short to revolve around one's work. Work is what I do, not who I am.

Personal & Professional

Personal/Professional Separated   Personal/Professional Intertwined

←————————————————————————————→

Personal matters should not be brought to work. Personal/family obligations should be scheduled around work. The personal and professional lives should and can be kept separate. The human factor is real but can't be indulged in the workplace. People won't understand if you plead a family emergency.

It is impossible to separate personal and family matters from work. You may have to interrupt work to take care of personal business. The personal and professional lives inevitably overlap. People will understand if you plead a family emergency.

Motivation

Professional Opportunity   Comfortable Work Environment

←——→

Professional opportunity and suc-cess are important motivating fac-tors. People want to learn, get ahead, move up in their professions or or-ganizations and have greater power, authority and responsibility. Job se-curity is not so important as the chance to make more money and advance in one's career.

People are motivated by the desire to have a pleasant work setting and good relationships with coworkers. Job security is imporant, as is an or-ganization that takes care of its em-ployees. Having more time off to spend with family is also very moti-vating. More power and responsibil-ity are not of themselves attractive, even if they mean more money.

—INSIGHT—

Americans and host country nationals may have different views of certain fundamental work-related topics.

The Key to Productivity

Results   Harmony

←——→

Focusing on the task insures success. People won't always get along, but you have to move forward anyway. Harmony is nice but results are what count. If you get results, people will be more harmonious. Getting results is ultimately more important than how you get them.

Working well with other people is the key to success in any enterprise. Harmony in the workplace will in-sure eventual success. Getting things done hinges on people getting along well. Results bought at the expense of harmony are too costly. How you get results is just as important as the results themselves.

The Ideal Worker

Technical Skills   People Skills

←——→

What matters most in a worker is his/her technical qualifications: edu-cation, work experience, and specific skills. "People" skills are important, but they don't contribute as much to the bottom line. Hiring a relative would be sheer coincidence and only if he/she had the skills you needed. Demonstrated competence is the key to getting promoted.

What matters most in a worker is his/her ability to work well with others and not rock the boat. Expe-rience and technical skills are impor-tant, but they don't contribute as much to the bottom line. Hiring a relative is always a good bet. Age and seniority are important for get-ting promoted.

CONTINUUM NOTES

If any two or three continuums show the host country and American positions at opposite ends, then indicate in the space provided how you think host country nationals perceive Americans in this respect:

Continuum: _____

How HCNs perceive Americans:

Continuum: _____

How HCNs perceive Americans:

Continuum: _____

How HCNs perceive Americans:

[For possible perceptions, see page 249.]

Observation Activity

4.10—OBSERVING THE WORKPLACE ✍

To complete this activity, you need to find someone working in the host country who will let you accompany him or her to the workplace for a day or a few hours for several days. Try to go on a day when a meeting is going on that you could attend. The person with you may be able to translate important exchanges for you if you aren't familiar enough with the local language, but even if there is no one to translate you can learn much about what's happening from your observations.

Your task is simply to watch and listen to what is going on around you and record what you see. Below are a list of questions to prompt or guide your observations. You don't need to answer these questions or use this list if you are more comfortable carrying out your observations in some other fashion. What is important is to take note of the differences between what you see here and what you would expect to see happening in a comparable workplace in the United States.

OBSERVATIONS

NONVERBAL COMMUNICATION

◇ How do people dress?

◇ How do they greet each other in the morning?

◇ What is the protocol for going in and out of someone's office?

◇ Do people maintain eye contact when they talk?

◇ How far apart do people stand?

MONO/POLYCHRONIC BEHAVIORS

◇ Do people come to work on time? Who does and who doesn't?

◇ What happens when someone who is talking to someone else gets a telephone call?

◇ What does a third person do when approaching two others who are already in conversation?

What did I know? I wasn't sure. And then it came to me: I knew how to get along with people. I knew how to bring people together. No, I didn't know a great deal about gardening or almost anything technical, but I was sure I could bring together those who did with those who wanted to learn.

—PCV Chile

◇ Do meetings start on time?

◇ How long do people with appointments have to wait?

POWER DISTANCE BEHAVIORS

◇ How do subordinates treat their superiors?

◇ How do superiors treat subordinates?

◇ Do you see evidence of bosses delegating authority or holding on to it?

◇ Do you see evidence of subordinates taking initiative, or just waiting for instruction?

◇ Whom do people eat lunch with? Do they eat only with their peers, or is there mixing of the ranks?

COMMUNICATION STYLES

◇ How is conflict handled?

◇ How is disagreement expressed?

◇ How is bad news or a negative concern communicated?

◇ How important does saving face seem to be?

◇ Are people generally direct or indirect in their conversation?

◇ Does this appear to be a high or low context workplace?

OTHER WORKPLACE NORMS

◇ When people interact, do they get to the task right away or talk more generally?

◇ Do people work closely together or more independently?

◇ Are women treated differently from men? If so, in what way?

◇ What kind of behaviors in workers seem to be rewarded? What are people praised for?

◇ What does the prevailing attitude seem to be about rules and procedures and the need to follow them?

What major differences do you see between this workplace and one where you've worked in the United States?

1. _____

2. _____

3. _____

4. _____

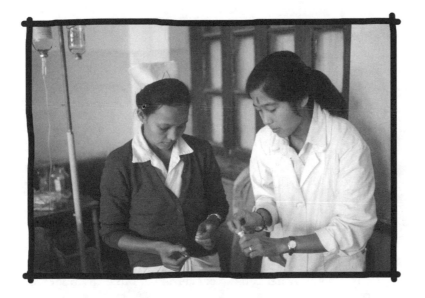

4.11—YOU AMERICANS ✍

Another issue you face in the workplace is dealing with some of the impressions your colleagues and counterparts have of Americans. Whether or not you actually contribute to these notions by your own behavior and whether or not you think they are fair or accurate, you can expect to run up against them. Below each of the eight common observations that follow, write a brief comment about why you think host country people might feel this way:

1. Why are you Americans always in such a hurry to get things done?

2. Why do you Americans insist on treating everyone the same?

3. Why do you Americans always have to say what you're thinking?

4. Why do you Americans always want to change things?

5. Why don't you Americans show more respect for your seniors and elders?

6. Why do you Americans always think things are going to get better?

7. Why are you Americans so concerned about individual recognition?

8. Why are you Americans so impatient?

[For comments, see page 249.]

Now select three of the statements on the previous page that struck you, for whatever reason, and answer the two questions given below:

1. Statement _____

    _____

    How would you feel if this statement were made about you?

    How would you respond if someone said it to you?

2. Statement _____

    _____

    How would you feel if this statement were made about you?

    How would you respond if someone said it to you?

3. Statement _____

    _____

    How would you feel if this statement were made about you?

    How would you respond if someone said it to you?

4.12—PACING 🌿

"What about the 'work?' You'll notice I put that word in quotation marks, not because you won't work very hard here. It's just that you won't understand why it's so hard. In the States, hard work is 60 hours a week. Here it's waiting for things to happen, watching them happen at a pace that's absurdly slow by the standards you're used to, and then trying to work the way the people work here. Otherwise you won't be working with them; you'll be working for them."

—PCV Madagascar

How good are you at waiting for things to happen?

How will you handle the slow pace at which things sometimes proceed in country?

4.13—TURNING THE TABLES ✍

PART ONE

To be effective working in another culture, it is useful to understand how you are being seen by your colleagues and counterparts. In the first part of this activity, you are asked to imagine that the tables are turned, that you are in the position of HCNs who are about to have a PCV join them in the workplace. To help put you in their place, imagine that you work in a typical American office, with ten or so coworkers, a supervisor, and an office head to whom the supervisor reports. All of you have worked together for at least a year and know each other and your respective jobs quite well. Now imagine that one day a person from another country shows up and begins working with you, someone who:

1. doesn't understand English very well, and speaks broken English that you can't always understand;

2. doesn't understand American culture or customs and is always making embarrassing mistakes;

3. doesn't understand his/her job very well and is not especially competent, at least in the beginning;

4. doesn't understand how things work around here; and

5. frequently behaves in ways that are insensitive, frustrating, or just plain rude.

How would you react to having such a person suddenly working in your office? Answer the following questions quickly and honestly:

1.	I would often find it frustrating.	Yes	No
2.	I would wonder why this person was sent to work here.	Yes	No
3.	I would not trust this person with anything important to do.	Yes	No
4.	I would assume this person didn't understand our system very well.	Yes	No
5.	I would imagine that working with this person would be more difficult than working with my other coworkers.	Yes	No

6.	I would be irritated at some of this person's behavior.	Yes	No
7.	I would think this person was insensitive.	Yes	No
8.	I would think this person had bad manners.	Yes	No
9.	I would find some of this person's behaviors very strange.	Yes	No
10.	I could never be sure what this person was thinking.	Yes	No
11.	I could never be sure how this person would react to something I might do or say.	Yes	No
12.	I would worry that this person could embarrass us.	Yes	No
13.	I would feel sorry for this person.	Yes	No
14.	I would find talking to this person frustrating and want to end the conversation as soon as possible.	Yes	No
15.	I would occasionally be hurt, insulted or frustrated by this person's behavior.	Yes	No

PART TWO

In the beginning of your tour, you will have to spend some time establishing your credibility. In thinking how you might do this try to recall other times when you were in a situation where you were an unknown or untested entity and had to prove yourself to others. What did you do?

1. _____

2. _____

3. _____

4. _____

5. _____

[For suggestions from other PCVs, see page 250.]

As the following statements indicate, however, some factors are working in *your favor*, and you may think of others to add to this list:

1. People assume that you wouldn't have come here if you thought you were going to be wasting your time. They can accept that *you* at least believe you have something to offer, which may make them think twice about you.

2. It may be known that whatever else you may lack, you do have the technical expertise to be here doing this job. You may never have done the work in this context before, but you do know your stuff.

3. The United States is seen as an advanced country in many respects, so Americans are often viewed as people who may have knowledge or experience that host country people do not have.

4. You are probably not the first PCV at this site. If your predecessors were even partial successes, then people realize that a PCV eventually can get things done.

5. _____

_____

_____

6. _____

_____

_____

—INSIGHT—

It may take some time before host country people start to give you the benefit of the doubt.

FROM JAN'S JOURNAL—AN ANALYSIS ✍

Now that you've finished this chapter, reread the excerpt from Jan's journal and note any additional observations/behaviors you now think are suspect; then read the analysis below.

Jan has experienced a number of the classic frustrations PCVs often encounter as they go about their work. Even so, she is probably being a little too hard on herself, as she seems to realize by the last paragraph.

Paragraph 1—

She laments her lack of progress, and then in the next breath says that a few people at the clinic do confide in her. She should be cheered by this fact, for it means she has made enough of a positive impression that certain people are sharing some of their innermost thoughts with her. Under the circumstances—she only goes there once a week, remember—this is progress.

Paragraph 2—

When she says she didn't talk to Mr. Beton when she first met him because "he was with a lot of other people," she is speaking like someone from a monochronic culture. If hers is a polychronic culture, she could probably have spoken to him in front of those other people (though not to complain or berate him) and not caused any problem. Indeed, she might never get a private audience with him, unless it is for something especially important.

When Mr. Beton's boss toured the clinic, Jan told her she wasn't getting any money for her work. This statement was ill advised, for several reasons. First of all, you don't normally tell big bosses your problems; you tell them what you think they want to hear and tell your immediate boss your problems. Worse, by going over Mr. Beton's head and complaining to *his* boss, Jan has committed a cardinal sin in high power distance/high uncertainty avoidance cultures: going around the chain of command. When Mr. Beton finds out, he will probably be quite upset, which may be why Jan hasn't gotten the meeting she requested yet.

Paragraph 3—

Designing a new sign-in form without being asked or without asking for permission—taking some initiative is what Jan would probably call it—is probably not a good idea in high power distance cultures. Bosses like to make decisions and don't like it when subordinates seize authority; in this case, Jan isn't even a subordinate but a volunteer. What's worse here is that this sign-in form may have been left to languish for a good reason: If money is based on clinic usage, then more tick marks (which is in the control of the secretary) means more money and is rather easy to arrange. But sign-in forms are less accomodating. Jan may wait a long time before her sign-in form ever shows up at the front desk.

Paragraph 4—

Jan says you can't just "wait around to be told what to do," like her colleagues. But in high power distance cultures, this behavior is the norm. Doing things without being told is usurping authority. She then says that at the staff meeting she mentioned she wasn't getting her money, so she had nothing to do. This statement might have been embarrassing to the man who handles volunteers or even to Mr. Beton, who will now look bad because Jan's project is going nowhere.

Paragraph 5—

She probably also embarrassed the deputy by asking in front of others when construction on the clinic was going to start. That it has not started could be perceived as a failing of the boss, and to have that failing brought out into the open could cause a loss of face. Another interpretation of this exchange might be that in the deputy's mind, to get to the point of breaking ground was a great achievement, representing considerable progress, and the fact that construction hasn't actually started yet is a minor detail. The hard work has been done.

To leave the world a bit better, whether by a healthy child, a garden patch or a redeemed social condition, to know even one life has breathed easier because you have lived—this is to have succeeded.

—Ralph Waldo Emerson

JOURNAL ENTRY 4

From what you have heard, what do you expect will be hardest about your job in the Peace Corps? How are you going to approach this difficulty? Has any of your previous experience prepared you for this problem?

FUNDAMENTALS OF CULTURE IV
THE LOCUS OF CONTROL ❧

This exercise introduces the fourth and last of the four fundamentals of culture: the locus of control. The two poles of this dimension, activism and fatalism, are defined and explored in the activity that immediately follows this one.

IV.1—WHO'S IN CHARGE HERE? ❧

Which of the following two statements do you most agree with? Circle one.

A. What happens to me is my own doing.

B. Sometimes I feel I don't have control over the direction my life is taking.

Percentage of Americans who chose A = 89%
Percentage of Chinese who chose A = 35%

What do you think accounts for the difference between American and Chinese percentages?

[After writing your answer, turn to page 251 for a brief discussion.]

—INSIGHT—

People from different cultures may see their ability to influence external events very differently.

IV.2—THE LOCUS OF CONTROL—
INTERNAL & EXTERNAL ॐ

Cultures differ greatly in their view of a person's place in the external world, especially the degree to which human beings can control or manipulate forces outside themselves and thereby shape their own destiny. The two sides of this dimension, internal and external control,* are described below:

Internal —
> The locus of control is largely internal, within the individual. There are very few givens in life, few circumstances that have to be accepted as they are, that cannot be changed. There are no limits on what I can do or become, so long as I set my mind to it and make the necessary effort. Life is what I *do*.

External —
> The locus of control is largely external to the individual. Some aspects of life are predetermined, built into the nature of things. There are limits beyond which we cannot go and certain givens that cannot be changed and must be accepted. Life is in large part what *happens to* me.

In the following sets of statements, circle the statement that does not belong, either because it is characteristic of internal control and all the rest are external control, or vice versa.

1. Stoicism is the rule.
2. The laws of the universe can be discovered.
3. Progress is inevitable.
4. Every problem has a solution.

1. Optimism is the rule.
2. Some things are a matter of luck or chance.
3. Where there's a will there's a way.
4. People believe strongly in technology.

*Based on concepts developed by F. Kluckhohn and F.S Strodbeck, <u>Variations in value orientations</u>, NY, Harper & Row, 1961.

1. Unhappiness is your own fault.
2. Progress is not automatic.
3. The workings of the universe are ultimately unknowable.
4. Nature cannot be dominated.

1. You make your own luck.
2. Some problems do not have solutions.
3. Where there's a will there's a will.
4. Unhappiness is a natural part of life.

(For suggested answers, see page 251.)

—INSIGHT—

Culture influences how much control people believe they have over their lives.

WHERE THERE'S A WILL

The scene is a cafe in Tangiers. Tomorrow is Saturday. I've just invited a Moroccan friend to a picnic at the beach. Will he come? "Perhaps," he says in English, translating from the Arabic, *N'Shallah*, which literally means if God is willing. I'm feeling hurt. What does he mean, perhaps? Either he wants to come or he doesn't. It's up to him. If he doesn't want to come, he only has to say so. He doesn't understand why I seem upset, and I don't quite grasp, "Perhaps." Our two cultures confront each other across the tea cups.

Only several years later, reading a book about culture, did I understand. He would come, he meant, if Allah willed it. His *wanting* to come and his being permitted to come were not one and the same. In Morocco, unlike America, where there's a will there is not necessarily a way. So who was I to demand an answer to my question? And who was he to give one?

It was an exciting moment. I had stumbled upon a parallel universe, one founded upon a different auxiliary verb, on *may* rather than *will*. Where there was one such universe, might there not be others?

—*PCV Morocco*

IV.3—SCORE YOURSELF—
INTERNAL AND EXTERNAL CONTROL ✍

Below are a number of paired statements (a. and b.). Immediately after reading each pair, circle which of the two best describes the action you would take or the way you feel about the particular topic.

1a. If I'm unhappy, I should do something about it.

1b. Nothing's broken if I'm unhappy; it's just part of life's ups and downs.

2a. The external world is a mechanism like other mechanisms; its workings can be discovered, predicted, even manipulated.

2b. The external world is complex, dynamic and organic. It cannot ultimately be known.

3a. You should see life as it really is.

3b. It is important to have a positive attitude about life.

4a. If I try hard enough and want something bad enough, nothing can stop me from getting what I want.

4b. Some things are beyond my reach, no matter what I do.

5a. What is new is suspect.

5b. What is new is usually better.

6a. I make my own luck.

6b. Many things happen because of chance or luck.

7a. Every problem has a solution, if you look hard enough.

7b. Some problems don't have a solution.

8a. I tend to be a stoic.

8b. I tend to be proactive and a doer.

9a. If a friend is depressed, I would try to cheer him/her up.

9b. If a friend is depressed, there is no need for me to do anything.

—INSIGHT—

Activists and fatalists live in very different worlds.

After making your selections, turn to page 252 for results, and then calculate whether you came out more on the internal or external side. Is your score here consistent with your self-concept?

IV.4—DOING

Americans are notorious for being doers, activists. One of the most common complaints of PCVs around the world is how long it takes to "get things done" in the host country. Sometimes the complaint appears in comments about the slow pace of life overseas. This American urge to do something, however, is somewhat inconsistent with the Peace Corps mandate to help *other people* do something. In your Peace Corps assignment, how do you think you'll be able to deal with this situation, to reconcile the activist side of your character? Will you have to redefine your notion of accomplishment or of success? Write your comments in the space below:

CHAPTER FIVE ⁕
SOCIAL RELATIONSHIPS

In this chapter you examine three of the most important social relationships PCVs have during their tour of duty:

↻ **relationships with host country families;**

↻ **friendships with host country people; and**

↻ **romantic relationships with host country partners.**

In a sense, your entire Peace Corps experience is nothing but a series of relationships with all manner of people in a wide variety of roles. All you have learned in this workbook about culture and cultural differences is only meaningful when applied in specific situations with specific individuals. This entire book, then, is really about how to handle relationships, both social and work related.

"Why," he said at last, "why did you come alone?"

"I thought it was for your sake that I came alone, so obviously alone, so vulnerable that I could in myself pose no threat, change no balance. Alone, I cannot change your world, but I can be changed by it. Alone, I must listen, as well as speak. Alone, the relationship I finally make, if I make one, is not impersonal, not political. It is individual. Not We and They, but I and Thou."

—Ursula Le Guin
The Left Hand of Darkness

5.1—DEAR JAN ⁊

In this letter from Jan's friend, Gavin, you find a lot of talk about friends and friendship. Mark any passages where you think Gavin has misunderstood or misinterpreted something that's happened or otherwise reached an incorrect conclusion:

Dear Jan:

1. Greetings from the East! Sorry you couldn't make it out in January, but there's still time. Shall I entice you with stories about what the sky is like out here, the colors of the sunset, the lushness of the hills? Maybe you'll feel more adventuresome later in the spring.

2. Speaking of adventures, there's certainly no shortage of them, is there? But they aren't the kind most of us expected, I think, at least not the kind I expected. I thought the hard part would be the bugs, the food, learning the language, and doing without TV. But that was easy. It's the people that are the challenge (and for whom I'm no doubt a challenge as well, as I remind myself when I'm being rational and objective, which isn't very often). I've made a couple of friends, I think, but I've got a lot to learn about friendship in this place. One of them, a guy I work with, invited me over for dinner last week, and as we were eating he asked me if I could "help" him with a problem he's having at work. I said sure and asked what it was. It turns out he wants me to lie for him about an incident that happened two weeks ago, when he said he had lost a report that in fact he just hadn't had time to write. The details don't matter, but I was shocked he would ask me this.

3. This same man can be very kind, too. I was a bit taken aback a few days ago when I happened to mention in conversation that my grandmother had recently passed away. I think he was hurt. He got a bit quiet and asked me why I hadn't told him sooner. He was very solicitous, asking if there was anything he could do. The next day he sent me a card—I guess they give these out at the church—announcing that he was having two masses said for my grandmother sometime next month.

(continued)

---

4. *Things at work are going as well as can be expected. The hardest thing to get used to is the casual attitude some people have toward their jobs. We were really busy last week, getting ready for the visit of the Minister of the Interior, and right in the middle of this, one of our key people suddenly disappeared for four days. When I asked where she was, someone said her cousin had died. I felt sorry, of course, but the cousin lived right here in the village, and I know the funeral took place on Monday, and this woman didn't come back to work until Friday.*

5. *Can you keep a secret? I think I have a girlfriend. I would say I knew I had a girlfriend, but it's a little hard to tell. She accepts my invitations to the movies or the pastry shop, but she always manages to bring someone else along with her, her sister, a best friend, once even her mother! We haven't held hands yet or kissed (is this getting too graphic for you?), but she did wear a pin I gave her. I'll keep you posted. At this pace, we might start using each other's first names before I complete my service.*

6. *Well, I could go on and on (and usually do in my mind), but it's time for my walk through the village. I started doing it for exercise (to the other end and back here takes 45 minutes), but now I do it as much for the show this place puts on. There's always something to learn or something new happening. I've decided that either this is a very interesting village or it's a very boring village and I'm one stimulus-starved individual.*

Cheers,
Gavin

5.2—The Circle of Relations ✍

As you enter the world of host country social relationships, you need a good map to guide you. This exercise asks you to construct such a map or chart showing how both you and your host country friends relate to and regard other people.

Part One

At right is a series of rings or concentric circles with you in the center. Look at the list of types of people which appears below and then place each type in one of the rings, nearer to or further from the center depending on any or all of the following criteria:

❧ how closely you are involved in that person's life and vice versa;

❧ how responsible you feel for the happiness and well-being of that person and vice versa;

❧ how much of your inner life, your most private thoughts and feelings, you share with that person and vice versa;

❧ how much that person "means" to you.

You may add other types of people and leave off any on the list that don't apply to you. Feel free to add to the rings if necessary or to draw your own chart if the placement of the rings doesn't suit you. Don't worry about being too precise; the idea is to get a *general* sense of the personal and emotional closeness you feel toward these people.

Your parents	Your grandparents
Complete strangers	Your first cousins
People you've met once or twice	Your closest friends
Your brother(s)	Your aunts and uncles
Acquaintances	Your second cousins
Good friends	Your children
Your spouse	Your in-laws
Your sister(s)	Your boss

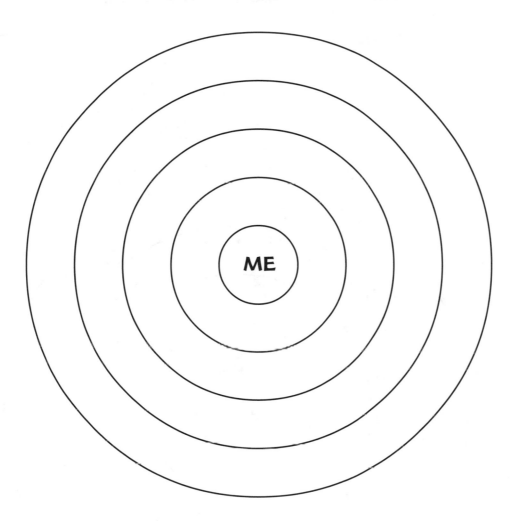

Part Two

You will now repeat this exercise from the perspective of a host country person. To do so you will need to find an informant, someone who knows the host culture well. Explain the activity and then ask that person to locate the various types of people on the chart reproduced below. When you have finished, compare your chart with that person's and then answer the questions on the next page.

—Insight—

Emotional and social distance from other people is greatly affected by culture.

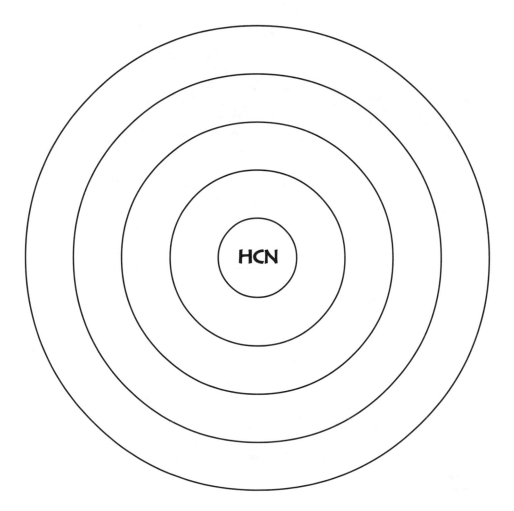

1. What are the most striking differences you notice between the two drawings?

2. What do you think accounts for these differences? (Discuss with informant if possible.)

> *The African family is large. Cousins and second cousins all fall under the heading of brother or sister, and uncles and aunts function as parents. If I were a student and wanted to study in Dakar, the assumption would be that I could live in the city with my extended family.*
>
> *—PCV Senegal*

3. Do you see any implications for your relationships with host country people?

5.3—RULES OF THE HOUSE—INTERACTING WITH A HOST COUNTRY FAMILY 🐍

Almost all PCVs form a close relationship with at least one host country family during their service. In this exercise, you consider some of the basics of living or being a guest in the host family's home. You have all been guests in people's homes before, but when you cross cultures, the rules may be different.

Below is a checklist of rules, divided into categories. However you can do so, find out about all the items listed below. Because some rules are gender and age based, try to talk to someone of your own sex and age and observe this person's behavior.

BATHROOM* ETIQUETTE

_____ How much time is it appropriate to spend in the bathroom in the morning when everyone is getting ready for the day?

_____ Are you supposed to lock the door when you're in the bathroom?

_____ How often is it appropriate to bathe?

_____ Which bathroom items are considered personal and which can be used by anyone?

_____ How clean are you supposed to leave the bathroom after bathing?

_____ What do you do with a dirty towel?

_____ Should you never do some things in the bathroom but in some other place that has a sink or running water?

_____ In the morning, do certain people always use the bathroom before others?

Think of any other rules of the bathroom you would tell a person from another country who was going to be a guest in your house back home. Do you need to find out about any of these rules here?

*Refers to a general area. This may also be a pit latrine.

EATING ETIQUETTE

_____ Is anything expected of you in getting the meal on the table?

_____ Where do you sit? Do you choose a place or wait to be told?

_____ Does a serving order exist?

_____ How much food should you take or accept when you're being served?

_____ When is it okay to start eating?

_____ What is the etiquette for getting a second helping?

_____ Do you have to eat everything on your plate?

_____ What is the etiquette for refusing more food?

_____ Should you talk during the meal?

_____ What topics should you talk about? What should not be talked about?

_____ Is it appropriate to praise the food?

_____ Is it appropriate to belch at the table?

_____ If you're not going to be home for a meal, do you have to let people know? How long in advance?

_____ What are the rules for inviting someone to a meal?

_____ When can you leave the table?

_____ Is it okay to take food or drink to your room?

_____ Is it okay to take food or drink to other rooms in the house?

_____ Can you help yourself to food from the refrigerator whenever you want to do so?

Think of any other rules of eating you would tell a person from another country who was going to be a guest in your house back home. Do you need to find out about any of these rules here?

HELPING OUT

_____ What household duties is a guest expected to help with?

_____ Is it appropriate to help with house cleaning?

_____ Are you expected to clean your own room?

_____ Are you expected to wash your own clothes?

_____ Are you expected to iron your clothes?

_____ Are you expected to take out the garbage?

_____ Are you expected to do food shopping?

_____ Are you expected to clean up after a meal?

_____ Are you expected to help prepare for a meal, e.g. set the table, put food on the table?

_____ Are you expected to help out with younger children?

Think of any other rules of helping out that you would tell a person from another country who was going to be a guest in your house back home. Do you need to find out about any of these rules here?

DRESS ETIQUETTE

_____ What dress is appropriate in the morning before you are ready to dress for the day?

_____ How should you be dressed when you are staying in the house and not going outside?

_____ What is appropriate dress for going to take a bath?

_____ How should you be dressed when you are in your room and the door is closed?

____ Are there rules about how you should dress for lunch and dinner?

____ How do you dress when guests are coming?

____ Can you wear shoes in the house?

____ For what occasions do you have to dress more formally?

____ In general, what parts of the body must always be covered, regardless of circumstances?

____ Is it okay to borrow clothes from family members?

____ Are you expected to lend your clothes to family members?

____ Is lending clothing to someone the same as giving it to them to keep?

I awoke to the faint sounds of small hands clapping three times, as custom requires upon entering a home.

—PCV Paraguay

Think of any other rules of dress that you would tell a person from another country who was going to be a guest in your house back home. Do you need to find out about any of these rules here?

PUBLIC AND PRIVATE

____ What rooms are considered public and which are private?

____ What is the etiquette for entering a private room?

____ What is the meaning of a closed door?

____ Is it okay to spend time by yourself in your room?

____ Are you not allowed in some areas of the house?

____ Are you expected to share personal possessions (tape player, books, cassettes, CDs, your laptop) with other members of the family?

We all obey numerous
rules for interacting with
people at close quarters,
most of which we aren't
aware of. The rules of
your host culture may be
different from what
you're used to.

____ What are the rules for bringing other people into
the house?

____ In what instances can you be in your room with
another person with the door closed?

____ When you leave the house, do you have to say
where you're going and when you'll be back?

____ What responsibilities do you have when other
guests come to visit?

____ Do you need permission to use such items around
the house as the TV, radio, sewing machine, and
other appliances?

Think of any other public/private rules you would tell a person from
another country who was going to be a guest in your house back home.
Do you need to find out about any of these rules here?

5.4—THE LIMITS OF FRIENDSHIP— WHAT DO FRIENDS ASK FRIENDS TO DO? ᕦᕤ

This exercise focuses on one key aspect of friendship: the responsibilities or obligations it incurs. If the requests below were put to you by a close friend back home, what would your answer be? If "yes," put a "Y" in the underlined space preceding the question; if "no," put an "N."

1. ____ Would you lend this person a substantial amount of money?

2. ____ Would you lie for this person in a situation where he/she was in trouble?

3. ____ Would you use your position or influence to help this person gain a special advantage over other people in getting a job in your organization?

4. ____ Would you serve as a go-between for this person in a difficult work situation?

5. ____ Would you let this person copy from your paper on an exam?.

6. ____ Would you intervene in a family or marital dispute if this person asked you to?

7. ____ Would you agree to take care of this friend's child for an extended period during a family/personal emergency?

8. ____ Would you look after this friend's house while he/she was away?

9. ____ Would you give a positive recommendation for this person if you did not think he/she would be good in a particular job?

10. ____ Would you help this person do something illegal if he/she asked you to?

Each night I sit with these four old men and learn their language. We go over simple phrases like, "How is the body? The body is well. I tell God thank you." But it is this small effort which brings us together.

—PCV Sierre Leone

Informant Activity

Ask a host country person, or someone who knows the local culture well, how he/she would answer these questions, and record the answers in the same way using Y or N.

1. _____ Would you lend this person a substantial amount of money?

2. _____ Would you lie for this person in a situation where he/she was in trouble?

3. _____ Would you use your position or influence to help this person gain a special advantage over other people in getting a job in your organization?

4. _____ Would you serve as a go-between for this person in a difficult work situation?

5. _____ Would you let this person copy from your paper on an exam?.

6. _____ Would you intervene in a family or marital dispute if this person asked you to?

7. _____ Would you agree to take care of this friend's child for an extended period during a family/personal emergency?

8. _____ Would you look after this friend's house while he/she was away?

9. _____ Would you give a positive recommendation for this person if you did not think he/she would be good in a particular job?

10. _____ Would you help this person do something illegal if he/she asked you to?

If you answered "no" to any of the questions to which the host country respondent answered "yes," how would you handle these situations if they actually were to occur?

—INSIGHT—

What friends expect of friends may be different in your host culture from what you are used to.

5.5—WHAT WOULD YOU DO? ⌬

In this exercise, you apply what you've learned about friendship in the previous activities to several specific situations. In the space below each of these incidents, note how you would handle them.

VISA PROBLEMS

You have become a close personal friend of one of the other teachers at your school. You have met her family and eaten at her house many times, and you have invited them to yours. You have also gone on numerous outings together. Today, as you sip morning coffee at your regular cafe, she asks you to help her get a visa to the United States. (She plans to go there, find work, and then bring her family over.) You reply that you know nothing about that and suggest she contact the American Embassy for information. "They are quite strict," she answers. "If you don't know an American who can help you, you don't have a chance." She asks you again if you would help. How do you respond?

GOING AWAY

You are very friendly with your next door neighbors, where you eat your meals on a regular basis. Today they inform you that the mother of the wife in the family has become gravely ill, and everyone is going to her town for what will probably be an extended stay— everyone, that is, but the youngest boy, 12 years old, whom the family does not want to take out of school. Instead, they would like him to stay with you and have you look after him until they return. You explain that you work all day and don't get home until the late afternoon, but they say that this schedule corresponds with his school schedule and wouldn't be a problem. From your knowledge of the culture, you know this is not an unusual request for close friends to make of each other, but you can't imagine looking after a 12-year-old boy for the next month. What can you say or do?

A PARENTAL VISIT

Your parents have just finished a whirlwind trip to your country, which did not give them time to visit the out-of-the-way and hard-to-get-to part of the country you live in. Accordingly, you met them in the capital and accompanied them on a two-day swing through the tourist hot spots. You have returned to your site after seeing your parents off and have recounted the story of their trip to your best friend, a colleague from work. When you finish, she's wearing a rather long face, and you ask her what's the matter. She says she would have very much enjoyed meeting your parents and feels hurt that you didn't think she was a good enough friend to introduce them to her. After all, she has taken you to her parents' house in the capital several times. How do you respond?

LOAN STAR

Two friends of yours in your village recently opened up a small grocery store. Things went well initially, but then their business dropped off. At this point, they asked you for a loan to help them get through the next two months. It wasn't much money, so you were able and happy to help out. Now they have come to ask you for more money, with the idea that their problem is their location. They have found a new place they could move to, but the owner of this new space wants a three-month advance on the rent, and your friends don't have it. You are beginning to suspect that your friends just aren't good businessmen and won't do any better at the new location than they did at the previous one. For this reason, and also because the sum they have asked for is quite substantial (though not beyond your means), you have turned them down. They are quite upset. "I thought we were friends," they say. "We would do this for you without a moment's hesitation. That's how friends treat friends in this country." Now what do you do? In retrospect, could you have done anything to avoid this situation?

MISSING FUNDS

You are very friendly with your neighbors, of which the father in the family happens to be a colleague of yours at work. They regularly invite you to meals, and you spend a lot of time at their house. Now, a most delicate problem has arisen at work. You have discovered, in your position as an accountant, that the father from next door has stolen money from the organization. You confronted him with your evidence, and he broke down and wept. He said he needed the money for an operation his youngest daughter just underwent and that he planned to put it all back over the next few months. He begs you to give him a chance and not tell anyone what you have discovered. He reminds you of all he and his family have done for you and asks for your trust. "Friends have to help each other in situations like this," he says. For your part, you know that if an audit is ever done of the organization's books, the missing funds will be discovered, and your own competence and credibility may be questioned. How do you feel about being asked to do this favor? What is your response?

[For brief notes on these incidents, see page 252.]

5.6—FAMILY LIFE ❧

Think for a moment about how various members of your host family interact with each other: husband and wife; parents and children; children and children; brothers and sisters; grandparents, etc. Do you see any differences in these interactions than that of the norm in the United States? Note what these are in the space below:

5.7—ROMANTIC RELATIONSHIPS ⟋⟍

The dynamics of romantic relationships are often puzzling enough in one's own culture, but even more complicated in an intercultural context. Even if you don't contemplate a cross-cultural romantic relationship during your Peace Corps tour, you may be the object of someone else's interest or you may unintentionally communicate interest in another person, who then responds. It is important, then, for you to be aware of any differences between the norms governing male/female (or same-sex) romantic relationships in American culture and those in your host country. To complete the first part of this activity (the "Me" side of the box), answer the questions below from the perspective of American culture. Feel free to add any other questions of your own.

PART ONE—AMERICAN PROFILE

1. How does a man show he is interested in a woman? (or another man?)

ME	HCN

2. How does a woman show she is interested in a man? (or another woman?)

ME	HCN

3. How does a man show he is not interested in a woman who *is* interested in him? (or in a man who is interested in him?)

ME	HCN

4. How does a woman show she is not interested in a man who *is* interested in her? (or a woman who is interested in her?)

ME	HCN

5. How do you know when the relationship is becoming something more than just friendship? What are signs that the other person is taking this relationship much more seriously?

ME	HCN

6. What do men/women do to show they want to pull back on or cool down the relationship?

ME	HCN

—INSIGHT—

Norms for romantic relationships are influenced by culture.

7. How much touching, embracing, and kissing is appropriate for a couple in public?

ME	HCN

Informant Activity

PART TWO—HOST COUNTRY PROFILE

Now ask someone who knows the host country culture well these same questions. Record the answers in the "HCN" side of the box next to those you have already written for yourself, and afterwards compare the answers. What are the most striking differences? What are the implications of these differences for having a romantic relationship in your host country?

5.8—MEN AND WOMEN— WHAT WOULD YOU DO? ✍

Below are a number of male/female criticial incidents. In the space that follows each description, write what you would do, based on what you know about romantic relationships in your host country. After you finish, you may want to discuss these incidents with a host country informant.

AFTER DARK

You enjoy your conversations with one of the other teachers at school and have gone together to a local cafe several times after class. Today you stayed longer than usual at the cafe and by the time you leave, it is after dark and your friend says he will walk you home. When you get to your house, you invite him inside to have something to drink. You get into another conversation, during which he moves closer to you and finally tries to put his arms around you and kiss you. You are very upset and start shouting at him. He is equally upset and says everyone knows what it means to invite a man into your house when you are alone, and you should stop trying to act so innocent. In retrospect, can you see how this misunderstanding could have occurred? Now what do you do?

WEDDING BELLS

You are an outgoing, vivacious, and warm person with a ready smile. You introduce yourself to people at social events and make them feel at ease. Last week, a shy, middle-aged widower at work asked you out to dinner, and you accepted and had a pleasant evening. He asked you again this week, and while you were somewhat hesitant, you accepted again. Now, today, he has sent you a beautiful card—containing a marriage proposal. You, by the way, are 24 and not interested in marriage. Now what? In retrospect, can you see how this misunderstanding could have occurred?

Just the Two of Us

You teach at an all girls high school in a large town on the coast. For the last several months, you have been dating a man you met at a school fundraiser. While you entered this relationship primarily because you were attracted to this man and enjoyed his company, you also thought it would be a way to enter more fully into the life of the local culture. But in this regard, the relationship has been a disappointment. He has not introduced you to his family or other relations nor to very many of his friends, except for a few male friends you have met on occasion. For the most part, you do things alone, just the two of you, and do not go to many public places, except for restaurants. Last night, you asked him again if you could meet his family, and he took your breath away with his response: "In our culture, men don't introduce their mistresses to their family. My wife would not be amused."

You are stunned; you had no idea this man was married and would never have gotten involved with him. You are very concerned that if word gets out about you, it could hurt your reputation at the school and even hurt the school's reputation. What now? In retrospect, did you have any indications that the relationship was not in fact what you thought it was? In future relationships, what would you say or do differently?

A TURNING POINT

You have been dating a host country woman for a few months, and recently she took you home to meet her family. After this family visit, the two of you slept together for the first time. Today when you meet, she starts talking about marriage and asks you what your plans are in this regard. When you reply that it's a bit premature to be even thinking, much less talking, along those lines, she becomes very upset. "You met my family and they approved of you," she says. "And we slept together. I thought you knew what that meant. We can't stop this now. Our family would be ruined." What can you say or do? Can you see what might have led to this misunderstanding?

PRESSURE

You have been dating a host country national for several weeks. You enjoy his company and you both like to do the same things. Through knowing him, his family, and his friends, you have gained a much deeper insight into the local culture. Recently, he has been pressuring you to have a sexual relationship with him, but for you, this represents a deeper commitment than you are comfortable making at this point. He says that in his culture, sleeping with somebody is not taken quite so seriously and asks you if you have something against him personally. You have assured him you do not. Now he has begun to accuse you of being a racist, saying that the reason you won't sleep with him is that he's an HCN. He has even told people at the place you both work that you are a racist (without giving any details), and you are starting to get concerned. What should you say or do? How could you have handled this situation differently?

UNREQUITED FEELINGS

One of the secretaries at work has had an obvious crush on you ever since you arrived at your post. While you are always friendly towards her, you do not have any romantic feelings for this person. Recently, she has accelerated her campaign and invited you to a couple of parties. You declined, knowing full well that she's interested in more than just a casual relationship. Your refusal has not gone over well, and she has retaliated for your rejection by spreading the rumor that you are sleeping with one of your 15-year-old students. What should you do? Could you have done something earlier to have prevented this situation from evolving to this point?

[For brief notes on these incidents, see page 252.]

DEAR JAN—AN ANALYSIS ᧞

Reread the letter to Jan at the beginning of this chapter and note any passages you now find suspect; then read the analysis below:

Paragraph 2—Gavin sees friendship largely through American eyes, which is only natural. Take his response to the friend who asked Gavin to lie for him: while such behavior is probably not something many Americans (certainly not Gavin) would consider asking of a friend, it may be well within the bounds of friendship in some cultures.

Paragraph 3—Gavin also interprets the next incident, concerning his grandmother, through American eyes. It does not appear that Gavin's grandmother has loomed large in his life. Like many American families, the grandparents may have lived some distance away and not been actively involved in Gavin's everyday life. Hence, his grandmother's passing away does not have so strong an impact on him. In the case of Gavin's friend, however, it is possible that several generations of the family inhabit the same household, or live close by, and the bonds between grandson and grandparent are as close as those between mother and son. The death of one's grandmother would be a major event—and one that Gavin should have mentioned immediately to someone he considered his friend.

Paragraph 4—This same cultural difference is at work in paragraph four. To Gavin, the death of a cousin, whom one might see once or twice a year at the holidays, hardly justifies four days off from work. But once again, the closely knit family structure in many cultures means that cousins might be as close to each other as brothers and sisters. Moreover, some cultures may expect more response at the time of a death than merely attending the funeral or sending a sympathy card.

Paragraph 5—Finally, regarding his girlfriend, Gavin doesn't make any mistakes here, as such, except to interpret all of her behaviors from his American point of view. It's true that in the United States, bringing your sister along on a date is unusual and might make one think this was something less than a date, but in Gavin's host country, for all he knows, it may be the norm. Accepting the invitation to go out may be a powerful message in that culture, more powerful than he realizes, and the significance Gavin assigns to holding hands and kissing may or may not be the same in the local culture.

People who go into the Peace Corps come back with some imagination. They aren't frightened when a Black runs for sheriff or something; they've seen Blacks run whole societies. They've seen Polynesians do just about as well in medicine as we do. People who have had this experience are set free by it.

—James Michener

MY MOTHER WANTS TO SEE YOU

One evening, very late, there was a knock at my door. It was rapid and continuous.

I yelled, "Shkoon?" (Who is it?)

"Besma," came the reply. "Fisa, fisa." (Hurry up.) I opened the door. "You must come over to my house right now, please."

"What's wrong"

"My mother wants to see you, and dinner is waiting." Although it was very late, I was accustomed to these impromptu invitations to meals at the Tounsi household. We walked hurriedly through the narrow streets, in and out of the complicated labyrinth of the *medina* to her neighborhood.

I was flooded with kisses by Besma's mother, Laila. She seemed especially excited to see me. She held my hand and escorted me through the courtyard into the family living area. The roomful of waiting people stood up to welcome me. I recognized almost everyone in the room as family and cousins. The only person not to greet me was an older gentleman who did not move from his seat but fixed his stare on me from the moment I came in the room. He seemed amused. Besma's mother once again grabbed my hand and led me to the couch. I was seated facing the stranger, and the room became very quiet.

Then the stranger started to speak. In perfect English, with a strong Arabic accent, he introduced himself as Uncle Mohammed. He gave me an abbreviated life story. He told me he was educated and that he took a degree in dentistry. He was financially secure and could promise me frequent vacations in Europe and a yearly trip to America to see my family. He explained that he had seen a picture of me, one that I had given to Besma. He knew the moment he saw it that I should be his wife. Did I accept?

Dumbfounded beyond words, I looked around the room. Everyone was perched on the edge of their chairs. I shot Besma a what-have-you-done-to-me look. When I turned to Laila, she was frantically nodding yes, yes, yes! I looked back at Mohammed, who was awaiting my favorable reply.

"How old are you?" I asked.

"Forty-six," he replied.

"Wow," was all I could say.

"It's a wonderful opportunity for you," he said, "really the chance of a lifetime." Then Laila chimed in. "You will be in our family. I am so happy." She was already congratulating me.

"Besma, can I speak with you a moment?" I asked. [The PCV speaks in private with Besma and then returns to the living room, all eyes upon her.]

"I'm sorry I cannot accept your gracious offer," I said. "My family wants me to marry a man from my hometown, someone I have known since my childhood." It was a blatant lie. "He is waiting for my return. I am here because I have so much yet to learn. I want to be ready for marriage, and right now I am not. I am too young. But when I am ready, it will have to be he who I marry."

"I understand," he replied. "Thank you."

—PCV Tunisia

JOURNAL ENTRY 5

What differences have you noticed in the friendships you have made with host country people and in those with fellow Americans? What has been the nicest part of living with a host family? The most difficult part?

FUNDAMENTALS OF CULTURE
COMPARING AMERICAN AND
HOST COUNTRY VIEWS ✑

In this activity, you are asked to identify the American cultural position on each of the four fundamentals (divided into eight topics) and then compare it to the host country position and to your own personal view. The mechanism here is the continuum on which you put a mark to identify the American (U.S.), host country (H.C.), and your own personal position (I) on this topic.

FUNDAMENTALS OF CULTURE—CONTINUUM

Self Identification   Group Identification

◄───►

Primary identification is with one's self. The self is the smallest unit of survival. Self-reliance, personal freedom, emotional distance from others are important. Protecting one's self guarantees well-being of others. Identity is a function of one's own achievements.

Identity is the function of group membership. The smallest unit of survival is the primary group. Interdependence, looking after the group insures well-being of the individual. People need close affiliation with others. Too much freedom is scary.

Egalitarian Mentality   Ingroup Mentality

◄───►

Egalitarian mentality is the norm. Group membership is casual & voluntary. No strong sense of in/outgroup exists. Most people are treated the same. People are informal with friends and strangers alike. It's easy to change groups and make friends.

An ingroup mentality prevails. People are close, intimate with their ingroup & compete with their outgroup. They're formal with all but their ingroup. People have little trust of their outgroup. Groups hardly change. It's harder to make friends.

Autonomous   Collective

←——————————————————————————————→

Autonomous organizations prevail. Workers are more independent. Individuals receive recognition & decision making is by majority rule. Loyalty from/to the organization is less; results are key & people are rewarded according to their contribution to the organization.

Collective organizations prevail. Teamwork, cooperation, group recognition & loyalty to/from the organization are the norm. Decision making is by consensus. Harmony is key. Rewards are distributed equally.

Universalism   Particularism

←——————————————————————————————→

Universalism is the rule. Personal & societal obligations are of equal importance and should be balanced. Rules should be applied equally to the ingroup & society in general. What is right is always right, regardless of circumstances. Objectivity is valued & expected.

Particularism prevails. It's necessary to distinguish between ingroup and societal obligations; the former are important, the latter less so. Being fair is to treat the ingroup well & let others fend for themselves. What is right depends on the situation. Context is crucial. Subjectivity is valued & expected.

Monochronic   Polychronic

←——————————————————————————————→

People's attitude towards time is monochronic. People must adjust to the demands of time; time is limited. Sometimes people are too busy to see you. People live by the external clock.

A polychronic attitude towards time is the norm. Time is bent to meet the needs of people. They're never too busy; there's always more time. People live by an internal clock.

One Thing at a Time

People do things one at a time. They stand in line; they expect undivided attention. Interruptions are bad; schedules, deadlines are important. Late is bad; adherence to schedule is the goal. Plans are not easily changed.

Many Things at Once

People do many things at one time. People stand in line less. Divided attention is okay. Interruptions are life. Schedules & deadlines are considered a loose guide. Late is late. Completing the transaction is the goal. Plans can be easily changed.

Life is What I Do

There are few givens in life, few things I can't change and must accept. I can be/do whatever I want, if I make the effort. My happiness is up to me. Unhappiness is not normal. Human beings are the locus of control.

Life is What Happens to Me

There are some things I have to live with; there may be limits to what I can do/be; happiness & unhappiness are normal parts of life. Human beings are only sometimes the locus of control.

Progress is Inevitable

Change is usually for the better. Tradition is not always right. Optimism is best. Technology is often the answer. Every problem has a solution. New is usually better.

Progress is Not Automatic

Change can be for the worse. Realism is best. Tradition is a good guide. Some problems can't be solved. Technology does not have all the answers. New is new, not necessarily better.

CONTINUUM NOTES

If the two cultures are at opposite ends on any two or three continuums, then in the space provided, be specific in describing how you think host country nationals would perceive you when they hold opposite views on this fundamental dimension of human behavior.

—INSIGHT—

American and host country views on some fundamental questions are quite different, meaning, of course, that their behaviors will sometimes be different too.

Continuum: _____

How HCNs perceive Americans:

Continuum: _____

How HCNs perceive Americans:

Continuum: _____

How HCNs perceive Americans:

[See page 253 for possible perceptions.]

182

CHAPTER SIX ⚘
ADJUSTING TO A NEW CULTURE

The focus in this chapter shifts from identifying cultural differences to learning how to live with them. The attention here is on the process people go through in adjusting successfully, both professionally and personally, to a new physical and cultural environment. You will be looking at three different aspects of this process:

  ✷ **the cycle or stages of adjustment**

  ✷ **the levels of cultural awareness**

  ✷ **changes in attitudes toward cultural difference**

In the latter part of the chapter, you will take a closer look at common adjustment problems of PCVs, at strategies for solving them, and how to cope with the stress that goes hand in hand with adjustment.

Adjustment poses a singular dilemma for many PCVs: in changing some of their behaviors to be more culturally sensitive, they turn into a person they no longer like. Is cultural sensitivity, at the expense of self-respect, too dearly won? It's a question many Volunteers struggle with through-out their tour of service and one that is treated in this chapter.

As you read through this material, try to remember that adjustment is not all struggle and no rewards. While it can be a trying experience, it's also challenging and enlightening, the kind of experience you would expect to have by joining the Peace Corps. If you approach the entire cross-cultural experience with your antennae out and plenty of humility, you will certainly be up to the challenge.

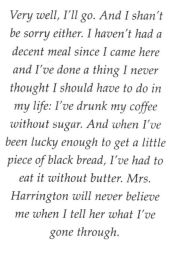

Very well, I'll go. And I shan't be sorry either. I haven't had a decent meal since I came here and I've done a thing I never thought I should have to do in my life: I've drunk my coffee without sugar. And when I've been lucky enough to get a little piece of black bread, I've had to eat it without butter. Mrs. Harrington will never believe me when I tell her what I've gone through.

Somerset Maugham
<u>*Mrs. Harrington's Washing*</u>

6.1—DEAR FRIENDS 🖎

Jan has been asked by Peace Corps to write a letter to people who have received an invitation to join the Peace Corps and serve in Jan's host country. In her letter, Jan has chosen to review her Peace Corps experience by looking back at the various stages she has gone through in adjusting to the country and culture, and reflecting on what it has all meant. Read this letter carefully; later in the chapter you will be asked to refer to it again.

Dear Friends:

1. The Peace Corps has asked me to write to you and tell you all about my country and my experience. I've filled several journals with what I think of this place and what's happened to me here, so you're not going to get very much in a two-page letter.

2. As you'll see soon enough, being here is such a rich experience, it's hard to stop talking about it—and harder still to know where to start.

3. I guess I could start at the beginning. When we got off the plane in the capital and it was so hot I thought there must be some sort of humidity alert, that everybody except for emergency workers had probably been told to stay indoors until this weather passed. I was wrong, of course; it was actually unseasonably cool that day, as I now realize, but that just shows you how far I've come. I don't even notice the humidity anymore, much less react to it.

4. Those were the days, though, when we couldn't get enough of this place. The people were the friendliest people on earth, and nothing we did seemed to faze them. After a while that changed, of course, and it began to dawn on us that one or two things about our culture appeared to be different from theirs, and that probably we shouldn't be quite so sure we weren't fazing the locals, since maybe they didn't "faze" the same way we did! It was all uphill from there.

5. Training is a kind of blur now, though I swore at the time that I would never forget anything that happened during those early weeks. I remember it was very intense—everything was intense in

(continued)

those days—and we were so incredibly busy all the time, that we couldn't wait for it to get over. On the other hand, we were scared to death that one day it <u>would</u> be over, and we would have to say goodbye and go out and become Peace Corps Volunteers.

6. But it did end, we did go out, and we did become PCVs— kicking and screaming in my case. I say that because my early days at my site and at my job were not my happiest moments. Even though I knew better, I made all the mistakes I had promised myself I would never make. I won't bore you with details, but suffice it to say that I thought I knew how to do things better than the local people, that if they would just listen, they would see the light and come around.

7. Once I realized I wasn't getting through, that they really did see things differently, I'm sorry to say I got a bit negative. If that's the way they wanted to do things, then to hell with them. This wasn't my finest hour. Somehow I had to climb out of this mood and get back on track. My first attempts were a bit clumsy. I told myself: "Okay, so these people aren't like you. Get over it!"

8. So I went back into the fray—and got bloodied all over again. This was starting to get annoying. I realize now that while I had accepted that the local culture was somewhat different from my own, I still thought that deep down inside we were all alike. While I might have to adjust my style, I didn't need to worry about my basic assumptions and life beliefs.

9. That was the biggest lesson I learned here: that cultural differences are not just on the surface, that people really do see the world in fundamentally different ways.

10. I don't want to say that everything you know about life and people goes out the window when you come here—that wouldn't be true, either—but culture does run deep, and so, therefore, do cultural differences. Anyway, I finally got wisdom, accepted that different people can see the same things very differently, and tried to be more understanding. Now I can laugh at those same behaviors that used to bother me—I've even adopted a few of them myself—and some of the things that bothered me I don't even see anymore.

(continued)

Remember that just as you judge from your cultural standpoint, you are being judged from theirs.

—PCV Fiji

11. *Well, I didn't expect to get so philosophic about all this, but I guess it's unavoidable whenever you start to look back. And I haven't told you anything about the country yet! I'll have to let others do that. After all, anybody can tell you about the markets and the busses, and the bugs and the food. But true insight—now that's harder to come by!*

12. *I want to say in closing that you'll notice I've addressed this letter to "Dear Friends." We've never met, of course, and probably never will, but I still feel that I know you—not your name or your face or any of the facts of your life—but your heart, or whatever you call that place where your values and your feelings reside. I know this much because I know myself, and I know that you must be something like me or it would never have occurred to you to join the Peace Corps and undertake this adventure.*

13. *We must hope for some of the same things, you and I, perhaps even for the same kind of world, where people understand each other better—where their first impulse upon meeting a stranger is to be curious rather than afraid. When I'm being sentimental (this is such a time, in case you haven't noticed), I like to think I have done my small part in making that happen. I sincerely hope you enjoy doing yours.*

All the best,
Jan

6.2—TRANSITIONS ✍

Adjusting to another culture basically involves two transitions:

- ✪ from living in one place to living in another place;

- ✪ from working in one job to working in a different job.

While describing the Peace Corps experience this way may make it seem less exotic or interesting, the fact is that for all the romance and adventure, it's probably not an entirely different kind of experience than you have ever had before, but rather a familiar experience (a transition) unfolding in a very *un*familiar setting (your host country). You may never have lived and worked in Poland or Papua New Guinea before, but you probably *have* moved and changed jobs before. In writing your answers to the questions that follow, think back to previous transition/ adjustment experiences in your life and try to remember any lessons you learned or skills you developed.

TRANSITION ONE—MOVING TO A NEW TOWN

1. What worried you the most as you prepared to move? Did this worry turn out to be accurate?

2. How long did it take before you were comfortable or content in the new environment?

3. Can you, in retrospect, identify any distinct stages in your adjustment to the new place?

4. Identify two or three specific things you did, consciously or unconsciously, that helped you to adjust in this new place.

5. What lessons from this experience can be useful to you now in the Peace Corps?

TRANSITION TWO—CHANGING JOBS

1.   What worried you the most about the job you were going to take?
     Did this concern turn out to be valid?

2.   How long did it take for you to become comfortable and compe-
     tent in the new job?

3.   Can you, in retrospect, identify any distinct stages in your
     adjustment to the new job?

4. Identify two or three specific things you did, consciously or unconsciously, that helped you adjust to your new job?

Expect to feel embarrassed, foolish, and sometimes inadequate. It's all part of the experience. These trying times are what we eloquently call "adjustment." They're difficult, natural, and useful.

—PCV Kenya

5. What lessons from this experience can be useful to you now in the Peace Corps?

6.3—THE CYCLE OF ADJUSTMENT ✍

As Jan's letter to her "friends" indicated, PCVs go through somewhat distinct stages as they adjust to their host country, the host culture, and their job. Together, these comprise the cycle of adjustment, during which PCVs' awareness of and attitudes towards cultural differences change and evolve. While the sequence of stages presented in this exercise seems to be true for most PCVs, no one Volunteer's experience is quite like another's. You may not have all the feelings and reactions described here, but you need to be aware of what *might* happen to you or your PCV friends as you move through your Peace Corps service.

I. INITIAL ENTHUSIASM (THE HONEYMOON)

Time frame: First week or two in host country

Characteristics: Exposure to country and culture is limited.

Excitement and enthusiasm abound.

Everything is exotic and quaint.

Attitude toward host country is generally positive.

Little is expected of you.

II. INITIAL COUNTRY & CULTURE SHOCK

Time frame: First few weeks; first half of training.

Characteristics: Wider exposure to country and culture means more realistic and more mixed reactions. Enthusiasm is tempered with frustration.

Feelings of vulnerability and dependence are common.

Homesickness is frequent.

Nothing is routine.

Limited language ability undermines confidence.

Close bonds are formed with other trainees.

III. INITIAL ADJUSTMENT

Time frame: Second half of training.

Characteristics: Routines are reestablished.

Some aspects of the country & culture are now seen as normal.

Adjustment to the physical aspects of the host country is better.

You are somewhat more self-reliant.

You are more positive about your ability to function in country.

Adjustment is to the culture of pre-service training as much as it is to host country culture.

IV. FURTHER CULTURE SHOCK*

Time period: First few months after training; settling-in period.

Characteristics: You experience post-training withdrawal symptoms.

You're adjusting to being on your own in country.

It's your first experience taking care of yourself in country.

You're having your first encounters with the work-related aspects of culture, with inital surprises and frustrations.

You miss daily contact with Americans and HCNs who understand you and your version of the local language.

You're surprised at still having culture shock to go through (you thought you adjusted during pre-service training).

V. FURTHER ADJUSTMENT*

Time period: Post settling-in.

Characteristics: You're getting used to being on your own.

You're better able to take care of yourself.

You're making friends in the community.

You speak the language better.

You're more effective at work because you under-stand the culture better.

In the underlined space that precedes each of the statements below, put the Roman numeral for the stage of adjustment you think the person was in who made the remark.

I.   Honeymoon

II.   Initial Culture Shock

III.   Initial Adjustment

IV.   Further Culture Shock

V.   Further Adjustment

1.   ____ I'm sick of these bugs.

2.   ____ I thought I knew this stuff!

3.   ____ You call that a toilet?

4.   ____ I'd give anything for a meal without rice.

5.   ____ These people are all so nice.

6.   ____ Homesick? For what?

7.   ____ I'm getting used to these toilets, believe it or not.

8.   ____ I'm looking forward to actually doing my job.

9.   ____ This language actually makes sense once in a while.

—INSIGHT—

Adjusting to a new
country and culture
happens over time.

10. _____ I don't believe it! They said I shouldn't jog here.

11. _____ Bugs? What bugs?

12. _____ You know, I actually *prefer* Turkish toilets.

13. _____ I'll never learn this language.

14. _____ Are you kidding? I can't eat curry (or beans) without rice.

15. _____ No one said my job would be like *this*!

16. _____ I never thought my problem would be *too much* free time.

17. _____ I actually prefer soccer to jogging; you meet more people.

18. _____ What a great place!

[For suggested answers and commentary, see page 254.]

*In the community-based model of pre-service training, there may be fewer differences between stages III, IV and V in the cycle of adjustment.

THE UGLIEST MAN

The rocks rattled and clanked as they rolled down the sloped zinc panels, raising a hell-sent cacophony that made my nerves jangle. I ran outside and chased the kids away, [but they returned, chanting] *"Timoteo, Timoteo, el hombre mas feo"* (Tim, Tim, the ugliest man) over and over again.

This unpleasant greeting set the tone for the first few months in my site. I organized soil conservation meetings that no farmers attended. I was heckled by wiry teenagers while giving presentations in my awful Spanish. With the help of school children, I planted a thousand baby trees around the Santa Rosa soccer field, only to find every single one of them uprooted and overturned a few days later. I had constant diarrhea, lost 20 pounds, and even the simplest tasks were a struggle to complete.

I knew my psyche had been scraped truly raw when one afternoon, coming home from a failed attempt to organize a tree nursery in a distant village, I was taunted by kids along the dusty hill path. It was the ever popular *Timoteo* chant that had quickly become my anthem, as far as the children of Santa Rosa were concerned. I saw red; the next thing I knew, I was chasing the little bastards up a hill waving my machete like a maniac, tears streaming down my cheeks and screaming in English: "I am not ugly, you little _____s! I am not ugly!"

—*PCV Guatemala*

There comes a day when all this suddenly becomes apparent, all at once. Things are no longer picturesque; they are dirty. No longer quaint but furiously frustrating. And you want like crazy to just get out of there, to go home.

—*PCV Peru*

6.4—SETTLING IN ✍

In many ways, life after pre-service training is very different from what you adjusted to as a Trainee, especially if your training follows the traditional as opposed to the community-based model. To understand what these diffrences might be, complete this exercise by checking any of the following statements that are *true* of your *pre-service training*.

1. ____ There is a large staff of people, as many as one for every three trainees, whose job it is to look after me.

2. ____ Most of the host country people I deal with have spent a lot of time before with Americans and are used to how they think and act.

3. ____ The host country people I deal with realize I don't understand very much about their culture and country and are quite forgiving of me.

4. ____ Most of the host country people I interact with understand my special way of speaking their language and understand me.

5. ____ Most of the host country people I interact with speak to me in a special version of their language used for people who are not very fluent.

6. ____ I spend a lot of my day speaking English.

7. ____ My day is full, well planned, and tightly scheduled.

8. ____ I have very little free time.

9. ____ Other people are taking care of me; I am expected to do very little for myself, so I can concentrate on all the things I have to learn as a trainee.

10. ____ I spend a lot of my time with other Americans.

As these statements are *not* going to be true of your life *after training*, if you checked all or most of them, then consider the following:

1. What are the implications of the fact that the host country people you have been dealing with use a special language with you and understand your special use of their language?

2. What are the implications of the fact that other people have been looking after you—food shopping, cooking, doing your laundry—and you've gotten used to being looked after in this way?

—INSIGHT—

You will have to do some adjusting after your training program ends.

3. What are the implications of the fact that you have gotten used to being around HCNs who already understand Americans?

4. What are the implications of the fact that you may have adjusted to the culture of pre-service training and not to the real culture?

6.5—THE LITTLE THINGS 🖎

"Not a single day passed without my painfully experiencing some Turk violating the "natural and logical way" of doing things. At first, it was staring, then it was abrupt "no" answers and arrogance from petty officialdom. Later it was blaring horns, and still later, continual interruptions while talking. Each little violation brought irritation, sometimes anger. Rapidly, these irritations built up into an explosiveness that was too easily provoked. This latent tension marred my stay in Turkey."

—***PCV Turkey***

Can you identify with what this PCV describes? Can you imagine it happening to you? Has it already happened to you?

How can you keep these little things from building up as she describes?

6.6—THE FOUR LEVELS OF CULTURAL AWARENESS ✐

As you go through the cycle of adjustment, your awareness of the host country culture naturally increases. This awareness tends to progress through a series of levels, which are described below,* with each level corresponding to a phase or phases in the cycle of adjustment.

I. UNCONSCIOUS INCOMPETENCE

This has also been called the state of blissful ignorance. At this stage, you are unaware of cultural differences. It does not occur to you that you may be making cultural mistakes or that you may be misinterpreting much of the behavior going on around you. You have no reason not to trust your instincts.

II. CONSCIOUS INCOMPETENCE

You now realize that differences exist between the way you and the local people behave, though you understand very little about what these differences are, how numerous they might be, or how deep they might go. You know there's a problem here, but you're not sure about the size of it. You're not so sure of your instincts anymore, and you realize that some things you don't understand. You may start to worry about how hard it's going to be to figure these people out.

III. CONSCIOUS COMPETENCE

You know cultural differences exist, you know what some of these differences are, and you try to adjust your own behavior accordingly. It doesn't come naturally yet—you have to make a conscious effort to behave in culturally appropriate ways—but you are much more aware of how your behavior is coming across to the local people. You are in the process of replacing old instincts with new ones. You know now that you will be able to figure these people out if you can remain objective.

IV. UNCONSCIOUS COMPETENCE

You no longer have to think about what you're doing in order to do the right thing. Culturally appropriate behavior is now second nature to you; you can trust your instincts because they have been reconditioned by the new culture. It takes little effort now for you to be culturally sensitive.

*This paradigm is based on work by William Howell.

—INSIGHT—

My understanding
of the local culture
and ability to
function effectively
will evolve over
time.

In the underlined spaces blow, write the Roman numeral(s) for the level(s) of cultural awareness you think the person making the observation is in. Some observations may go in more than one stage.

1. _____ I understand less than I thought I did.

2. _____ These people really aren't so different.

3. _____ There is a logic to how these people behave.

4. _____ Living here is like walking on eggshells.

5. _____ These people have no trouble understanding me.

6. _____ It's possible to figure these people out if you work at it.

7. _____ I wonder what they think of me.

8. _____ I know what they think of me.

9. _____ It's nice to be able to relax and be myself.

10. _____ I'll never figure these people out.

11. _____ Why did people say this would be so difficult?

12. _____ There's hope for me here.

[See page 254 for suggested answers.]

6.7—ATTITUDES TOWARD CULTURAL DIFFERENCE—FROM ETHNOCENTRISM TO ETHNORELATIVISM ॐ

In this activity you look at another aspect of adjustment: attitudes toward cultural difference. As your awareness of culture increases, your attitude toward cultural difference likewise evolves. The model summarized below by Dr. Milton Bennett describes this journey from ethnocentrism to ethnorelativism:

ETHNOCENTRISM

STAGE I—DENIAL

People in this stage don't really believe in cultural differences; they think people who are behaving differently don't know any better. These people tend to impose their own value system on others, knowing that they're "right "and these other people are "confused." They believe the way they behave is natural and normal and the way other people behave, if it's different, is wrong and misguided. These people are not threatened by cultural differences because they simply don't accept them. Generally, people in this stage have had limited contact with people different from themselves and thus have no experiential basis for believing in other cultures.

STAGE II—DEFENSE

These people have had an indication that their value system may not be absolute—and they're not happy about it. Unlike people in the denial stage, those in the defense stage believe in cultural difference and have accepted the reality of it, but they are deeply threatened by it and believe that other cultures are decidedly inferior. "This may be how things are, but it is not the way things *should* be." They know better than to try to impose their values on others, but they view other cultures negatively and prefer to have little or no contact with those who are different.

STAGE III—MINIMIZATION

People at this stage are still threatened by difference—that's why they try to minimize it—but they don't think that those who are different are inferior, misguided, or otherwise unfortunate. Rather, they believe that the differences are real but not especially deep or significant, that as different as people are, they are still more similar than dissimilar. We are different on the surface, but underneath we share many of the same values and beliefs. If people in the denial stage deny difference and people in the defense stage accept but demonize difference, then people in the minimization stage try to trivialize difference.

ETHNORELATIVISM

STAGE IV—ACCEPTANCE

These people accept differences as being deep and legitimate. They know other people are genuinely different from them and accept the inevitability of other value systems and behavioral norms. They still find some of these behaviors hard to deal with or accept, but they are not threatened by them nor do they judge them as wrong or bad. They do not normally adopt many of these behaviors for themselves nor necessarily adjust their own behaviors to be more culturally sensitive, but they have a more tolerant and sympathetic attitude. They are neutral, not positive, about differences. Difference is a fact of life.

STAGES V & VI—ADAPTATION AND INTEGRATION

In these stages, behavior as well as attitudes change. These people have gone from being neutral about difference to being positive. They not only accept cultural differences, but are willing and able to adjust their own behavior to conform to different norms. They are able to empathize with people from different cultures. In many ways, they become what is known as bicultural or multicultural, effortlessly adjusting their behavior to suit the culture of the people they're with, "style switching," in other words. They do not give up their own or birth culture's values and beliefs, but they do integrate aspects of other cultures into it. In the integration stage, certain aspects of the other culture or cultures become a part of their identity.

PART ONE

For each of these stages, answer the following questions.

I. DENIAL

1. Can you think of anyone you know who is in this stage?

2. Have you ever exhibited any of the behaviors associated with this stage? If yes, briefly describe.

II. DEFENSE

1. Can you think of anyone you know who is in this stage?

2. Have you ever exhibited any of the behaviors associated with this stage? If yes, briefly describe.

III—MINIMIZATION

1. Can you think of anyone you know who is in this stage?

2. Have you ever exhibited any of the behaviors associated with this stage? If yes, briefly describe.

Adaptation comes out of encounters with novelty that may seem chaotic. In trying to adapt, we may need to deviate from cherished values, behaving in ways we have barely glimpsed, seizing on fragmentary clues.

—Mary Katherine Bateson
<u>*Peripheral Visions*</u>

IV—ACCEPTANCE

1. Can you think of anyone you know who is in this stage?

2. Have you ever exhibited any of the behaviors associated with this stage? If yes, briefly describe.

V & VI—ADAPTATION AND INTEGRATION

1. Can you think of anyone you know who is in this stage?

2. Have you ever exhibited any of the behaviors associated with this stage? If yes, briefly describe.

↻ In general, what stage do you think you are in now? Why do you think so?

↻ How did you move from the stage or stages you were in before to the stage you are in now?

↻ Consider for a moment two or three PCVs you have met in this country and know fairly well. What stages are they in? Are they all in the same stage? What do you think accounts for any differences?

PART TWO

Reread Jan's "Dear Friends" letter at the beginning of this chapter. At various points in this letter, Jan describes certain behaviors or attitudes that clearly place her in one or the other of all six stages outlined on pages 201 and 202. In the exercise below, you are asked to match each stage with a paragraph from her letter:

I. Denial .... Paragraph # _____

II. Defense .... Paragraph # _____

III. Minimization .... Paragraph # _____

IV. Acceptance .... Paragraph # _____

V. & VI. Adaptation & Integration .... Paragraph # _____

[Turn to page 256 for suggested answers.]

A DIAGRAM OF CULTURAL ADJUSTMENT

All of the previous exercises have been examining one or another of three aspects of cultural adjustment—the adjustment cycle, the levels of cultural awareness, and the attitude toward cultural difference. Although examined separately, they are all features of the same phenomenon. The graphic below shows you how these three models or dimensions of adjustment fit together.

For certain stages of the cycle, more than one level of awareness or attitude toward difference may be listed. For certain aspects of the culture, the PCV or trainee may be at one level, and at another level for other aspects. For example, you might be consciously incompetent (in the initial adjustment stage) regarding some aspects of the culture but consciously competent regarding others and be minimizing certain aspects of difference, accepting others, and adapting still others.

Further Adjustment

Conscious Competence & Unconscious Competence

Acceptance, Adaptation, Integration

Initial Adjustment

Conscious Incompetence & Conscious Competence

Minimization, Acceptance, Some Adaptation

Initial Enthusiasm

Unconscious Incompetence & Conscious Incompetence

Denial, Defense, Minimization

Further Culture Shock

Acceptance, Adaptation

Conscious Competence

Initial Culture Shock

Conscious Incompetence

Defense, Minimization

6.8—THE TOUGHEST PART 🐾

"I had mistakenly expected the toughest part to be getting used to the physical conditions, but I soon realized the hardest part is the emotional adjustment. Getting used to the slow pace of life, the isolation, and living in a fishbowl—these all take time."

—*PCV New Guinea*

How do you think you will adjust to the slow pace of life?

How will you adjust to living in a fishbowl?

6.9—COPING STRATEGIES 🐍

Living and working in another country, especially in the beginning, is a series of stressful events, interspersed with occasional periods of calm. For the most part, this stress is the result of the myriad adjustments you have to make, from the trivial to the profound, as you do the following:

- ✪ learn new ways of doing things;

- ✪ learn to do things you've never done before;

- ✪ stop doing things you can no longer do;

- ✪ adjust to an entirely new set of people;

- ✪ learn to live and work in an environment where you speak a foreign language;

- ✪ get used to various new and unusual phenomena;

- ✪ learn to live without all kinds of familiar phenomena.

Everyone has experienced stress before and has developed strategies for coping with it. This exercise is designed to remind you of some of your strategies and to help you think of others you may find useful in your new setting. Under the five categories listed on the next page, write your ideas and suggestions for what you can do to cope with stress.

Notice that "Ways I Can Improve My Language Skills" is listed as its own category. Strictly speaking, improving your language skills is simply one more coping technique that could fall under the category of Things I Can Do On My Own, but it is such an important technique, with so many specific possibilities, that it has been given a place of its own. An example is under each category.

THINGS I CAN DO WITH OTHER PEOPLE

Invite people over

_____

_____

_____

_____

_____

_____

_____

THINGS I CAN DO ON MY OWN

Read

_____

_____

_____

_____

_____

_____

_____

THINGS I CAN REMIND MYSELF OF

This will pass

_____

_____

_____

_____

_____

_____

_____

WAYS I CAN IMPROVE MY LANGUAGE SKILLS

Talk to children

_____

_____

_____

_____

_____

_____

THINGS I HAVE ALREADY DONE HERE IN-COUNTRY

_____

_____

_____

_____

_____

_____

SUGGESTIONS

Here, for your reference, is a list of coping strategies compiled from suggestions of PCVs from around the word:

THINGS I CAN DO WITH OTHER PEOPLE

Invite people over
Go and visit someone
Telephone someone
Go to a movie, cafe, etc. with someone
Play a game with someone
Participate in a team sport
Volunteer my services to a needy cause

Stress affects everyone at one point or another and is indeed the biggest health problem. But it's always worth it. The frustrations, disappointments and heartaches are made up for by the fascinations, euphorias, and revelations.

—PCV Papua New Guinea

THINGS I CAN DO ON MY OWN

Read	Play cards
Listen to music	Cook a meal
Take a walk	Meditate
Go to a movie	Write in my journal
Go to a restaurant or cafe	Go shopping
Exercise	Listen to the radio
Garden	Take some pictures
Call home	Look at photos
Write letters	Make a tape to send home
Play an instrument	Take a ride
Solve puzzles	Watch birds
Practice a craft	Take a trip
Watch television	Watch people
Study language	Deep breathing

THINGS I CAN REMIND MYSELF OF

This will pass.
It's not the end of the world.
I came here to experience a challenge.
I've been through worse than this.
It's natural to feel down from time to time.
No pain; no gain.
It's not just me.
Things didn't always go well back home either.
I have taken on a lot; I should expect to feel overwhelmed from time to time.

WAYS I CAN IMPROVE MY LANGUAGE SKILLS

Talk to children
Talk to older people (who have more time and patience!)
Go to a cafe and eavesdrop
Listen to the radio or TV
Join a club or sports team
Participate in some other kind of group activity
Study a language textbook
Do exercises in a language textbook
Listen to language tapes
Ask a host country informant to tape record key language phrases that I can practice.

6.10—Can I Still Be Me? ✍

The Peace Corps experience has a number of built-in dilemmas, but none more significant than the question of how one adjusts to a different culture and still maintains one's own values, identity and self-respect. On occasion, the behavior expected of you by the local culture may conflict with your own personal values and beliefs. Do you adopt the behavior and think less of yourself, or do you resist it and risk being considered insensitive? Fortunately, in many cases, it is not an either/or choice, but when it seems to be, what do you do?

Reading, reflecting and commenting on the incidents below, which could happen in any culture, may help you handle such situations. You also may want to talk with one or two PCVs to find out what they have done in similar circumstances, how they managed to be culturally sensitive *and* true to themselves at the same time.

Holding Back?

You are a female PCV working as an environmental educator in a government ministry. You work under an older host country man who is much less technically competent than you. At staff meetings, you routinely outshine this man, which has begun to cause him acute discomfort. Today he has asked you not to speak at these meetings and especially not to contradict or disagree with him when he speaks, even (and especially) if what he says is incorrect. What should you do?

Drawings

Part of your job as a PCV urban planner is to review and sign off on staff draftsmen's drawings before they are sent on to higher management. Your division has just hired a new draftsman who is incompetent but is a cousin of the head of this division. Tomorrow you will be reviewing the first of his drawings, and this afternoon your supervisor has called you into her office. She says you can expect these drawings to be of an unacceptable quality but asks you to approve them anyway. She doesn't want any trouble with her boss or to unnecessarily embarrass the young man. How would you respond?

I have realized that for survival, I need to be more assertive, but only to a certain point. Some things are completely unimportant and I can let them go, but I have also obtained the courage to speak out if I am feeling violated or taken advantage of.

—PCV Guniea-Bissau

FRIENDLY ADVICE

You teach school in a rural part of your country. You eat your meals at a local tea shop run by a low-caste family with whom you have become very friendly. Today the headmaster of your school has approached you and advised you to stop eating at this place. He says it hurts your social standing and indirectly hurts the reputation of his school for you to be seen so often in the company of untouchables. What do you do?

GOOD NEWS

You have been conducting an evaluation of a year-old pilot agricultural extension project. During the course of your study, you have discovered a number of irregularities, including serious misuse of funds, and, in general, have found that the project has been almost a complete failure. In the report you just finished, you have recommended that no further funds be spent. This morning your supervisor has come to you and pointed out that the state senator for this district, who is running for re-election, needs some good news to jump start his campaign. A favorable report on the project would be very useful, not just to the candidate, but to your boss and, ultimately, to the organization you work for. He asks you to rewrite your report. What do you do?

Since you left, nothing is like yesterday. We kept your memories in our heart because you taught us with love. And when you give love, you receive the same thing—love.

—Letter from HCN to PCV Venezuela

EXTROVERT

You are an outgoing, gregarious woman, interested in people and naturally friendly. Today your boss has called you into his office and explained that your friendliness has been remarked upon and is causing misunderstanding in certain quarters. The women who work in the office think you are acting flirtatious, even loose, and the men have begun to question your professionalism. Your boss asks you if you can "tone it down" a bit. You are hurt and surprised; this is just the way you are. What do you say or do?

AWAY FROM HOME

You are a community development worker, helping install an irriga-tion system in the provincial capital. You, your host country supervisor, and a team of eight technicians have been living here for three weeks in one of the local guesthouses. Away from their families, these men have shown a side of their personality you have not seen before. They start drinking as soon as they get back from the site, about ten miles from town, and at least once a week they visit the town's red light district. They always invite you to these "events," but as you neither drink nor care to visit prostitutes, you have been declining. You can see that your consistent refusals are beginning to create a gulf between you and them. What do you say or do?

JOURNAL ENTRY 6

What do you think will be especially difficult for you to adjust to in your host country? What has been hardest so far for you to get used to? What are some of the enjoyable aspects of being in your host country that are going to compensate for some of the difficulties? What qualities do you think are important for adjusting to life as a PCV? Do you have these qualities?

APPENDIX ✌
CONTINUING YOUR LEARNING

The exercises in this appendix are meant for you to do after you finish your training and go out to your site. Once there, you become immersed in the culture, living and working in it, puzzling everyday with some cultural enigma or other. These activities encourage you to step back for a moment and once more study the culture deliberately and systematically. They complement the workbook exercises and provide you with techniques for studying culture that can be repeated and referred to often during your service and when you return home.

Of the gladdest moments in human life, methinks, is the departure upon a distant journey into unkown lands. Shaking off with one mighty effort the fetters of Habit, the leaden weight of Routine, the cloak of many Cares, and the slavery of Home, man feels once more happy. The blood flows with the fast circulation of childhood. Afresh dawns the morn of life.

—Sir Richard Burton,
The Devil Drives

1—USING CULTURAL INFORMANTS ॐ

One way to continue learning about your host culture is to identify people who understand it and can explain it to you. In general, you look for information of three kinds:

1. important facts or textbook information about the culture;

2. ways to behave and not behave in various situations; and

3. reasons for host country people's behavior or reactions.

You may need to approach different informants for these different kinds of information. In most Peace Corps posts, you have your choice of four types of potential informants:

1. host country nationals;

2. other Peace Corps Volunteers;

3. other Americans (not PCVs); and

4. third-country nationals.

You might assume that host country nationals will always be your best resources, but this may not necessarily be true. They may know the do's and don'ts of host country behavior, but not all may know many facts about their culture, nor *why* host country people behave the way they do. For this information, you may be better off asking foreigners or that handful of host country people who have studied their culture.

GUIDELINES

In dealing with informants, keep the following general guidelines in mind:

1. Critically evaluate the opinions of PCVs, other Americans, and third-country nationals who seem especially negative or bitter about the host culture.

2. Select people who have been in the country long enough to have successfully built relationships and have some perspective.

3. Select host country people who are somewhat representative of their country:

   ↻ Avoid those who may be too Westernized, or at least consider their Western bias in evaluating their comments.

   ↻ Remember that people who speak English may not be representative of the general population.

   ↻ Your Peace Corps trainers or other HCN staff also may not be especially representative (though they may be knowledgeable and understand where you're coming from).

4. Talk to a variety of informants, a cross section, so you don't get the views of just one social class, one ethnic group, only men, the college educated, etc.

5. Try to corroborate what you've heard from one informant with the views of at least one other person.

6. Try to select informants who are objective, able to distinguish between their own personal experience and what is true of the culture in general. Otherwise, *you* have to do the distinguishing.

It may be interesting for you to see how the views of the four types of informants compare by asking each of them the same question. These are some suggestions:

1. Why do host country people _____ ?

2. How should I treat counterparts at work?

3. Someone asked me to lend them money. What should I do?

4. Is it okay in this culture to _____ ?

2—Joining In ☙

Perhaps the most natural way of learning about the culture around you is to actively participate in it, to become involved in the life of your community and its people. Much of this involvement happens automatically as you go about living and working in your village or city, but you can also make a conscious effort to become involved in community activities outside your work and meet people you ordinarily would not. The easiest way to become involved is through a friend or host family member who is already engaged in an activity that might interest you. Below are some suggestions:

1. Donate your time and services as a volunteer to any organization, public service, or institution that accepts volunteers, such as any of these:

    ✿ a hospital or clinic;

    ✿ nursing home;

    ✿ a local charity.

2. Offer to teach English in any venue where it seems appropriate.

3. Offer to teach any other skill you have that people might be interested in learning.

4. Become a member of the congregation of a local church.

5. Join a church group in that church.

6. Join or start a choir or some other singing group that meets regularly.

7. Join or start a group that plays music.

8. Offer to tutor students at the local school, or start a tutoring program.

9. Join an existing women or men's club, or start one

10. Join a local sports team.

11. Join any interest group that meets regularly—a sewing class, pottery class, poetry group, self-defense class, bird-watching club, video club—or help to start one.

12. Help to organize a special event such as these:

    ♻ a fund raiser;

    ♻ a craft fair;

    ♻ a beautification project;

    ♻ a painting project;

    ♻ a construction project;

    ♻ a local library cleanup;

    ♻ an environmental cleanup.

13. Offer to help out with a local boys' or girls' club.

14. Join an organization affiliated with your workplace.

15. Help to organize field trips for school children, people in a nursing home, or a boys' or girls' club.

If you're at a loss about getting started, ask other people how they did it.

3—Keeping a Journal ✍

Many of the other techniques for continued learning presented in this module imply the regular use of a journal. Keeping a journal provides you the opportunity to reflect on your experience and to stay in tune with your emotions and feelings, and to refer back to when you decide to explain your experience to an audience back home. A journal illustrates the work-in-progress that is your Peace Corps experience, recording your deepening understanding of the culture around you and the changes that are taking place in you as you adjust to your host country. It is a record of your struggle to come to grips and make your peace with the strange, foreign reality that slowly becomes your home.

Most PCVs find they use journals for a number of different purposes:

- to make random notes;

- to think out loud (on paper);

- to record the events of the day;

- to record a conversation;

- to record observations, random or targeted;

- to record impressions and reactions;

- to relate events and experiences (to tell a story);

- to record thoughts and emotions;

- to record realizations and conclusions;

- to write poetry or fiction;

- to talk to themselves.

THREE COMMON MISTAKES

1. If you associate writing in your journal with an hour of serious thinking and literate prose, chances are you'll be too daunted to ever begin. Start simple, recording a few thoughts, ideas, questions in a 10-to-15-minute respite at the end of the day.

2. Don't think of your reader or your writing style. Write for yourself, not posterity; otherwise, you edit too much and stop the free flow of your thoughts and emotions while they're happening.

Men and women confronting change are never fully prepared for the demands of the moment, but they are strengthened to meet uncertainty if they can claim a history of improvisation and a habit of reflection.

—Mary Catherine Bateson
Peripheral Visions

3. Don't delay your writing for more than a day. It's only when you haven't written for two weeks or so that you find yourself spending two hours, feeling exhausted and negative towards what has become a chore. It's also better to write when things are fresh in your mind, and you can recall details.

If you haven't started already, in a notebook where you write nothing else, begin writing. For the first few weeks, just describe what's been happening. It's automatic and customary to interpret and categorize, but that can come later as you reflect on what you've written in light of what you now know about the culture. By their very nature, frustrating experiences are only understood in retrospect, upon reflection and analysis—and cultural adjustment is full of just such experiences.

You may want to organize your journal in this way:

Observation/Description	Opinion/Analysis/Judgement
On this side of the journal, describe what you saw. Anything that strikes you as different, funny, weird, sad, etc. is appropriate. Feelings, emotions, judgments should not be expressed on this side. Just stick to the facts.	*On this side of the journal, describe your thoughts, feelings, etc. about the event. Then try to analyze why you feel this way. What in your cultural makeup may be affecting how you feel? How is it different from whatever values or assumptions may be at work in the new culture?*

4—Learning From The Media and The Arts ✍

In every country, a great deal about the culture is revealed by the media, which includes the following:

- ❧ **Books/Poetry;**
- ❧ **Newspapers;**
- ❧ **Magazines;**
- ❧ **Radio;**
- ❧ **Television;**
- ❧ **Movies/Theater;**
- ❧ **Songs and music.**

Your ability to use the media to learn about the culture depends on how well you speak and read the language, but even if your local language skills are minimal, you have some options.

I. Books/Poetry

1. Try to find English translations of the most famous works of the best known authors in your country. You may be able to find a translation locally, or ask your family back home to look for one.

2. If no translations are available, ask an informant to tell you about some of the great works of literature in his or her country, including the plot and important themes of these works.

3. Go to the local bookstore (ideally with an informant) and look over the selection. What books are the most popular? Which subjects have the most books devoted to them? What subjects aren't covered or are barely covered?

II. Newspapers

1. Does the country have an English language paper? If so, read it regularly for insight into numerous aspects of the country and culture.

2. If no local English language paper exists, look with an informant at other newspapers and see which stories get the most space and what is relegated to the inside. What different sections does the newspaper have, and who is the intended audience for each one?

III. MAGAZINES

1. Read any local English language magazines you can find.

2. If none exist, sit down with an informant and "read" a host country magazine from time to time to find out what topics are discussed and what is said.

3. On your own, study the advertisements and pictures in magazines.

4. Go to the magazine section of your local newsstand or bookstore and see what kinds of magazines are there. Which topics or areas of interest have the most magazines devoted to them? What topics are missing?

IV. RADIO

1. Listen to any locally or regionally produced programs in English.

2. Listen to the radio with an informant. Select different types of programs—news broadcasts, public affairs programs, dramas, interviews, etc.—and ask your informant to relate the content. Ask him or her which are the most popular programs and why. Ask who listens to the radio and when they listen.

V. TELEVISION

1. Watch locally or regionally produced television, whether you understand the language or not. (It's an excellent way to improve your language skills.) What kind of shows are the most common? What kinds of stories, people, events are depicted?

2. Watch TV with an informant and ask questions about what you're seeing. In dramas, how can you tell who are the good guys and the bad guys?

3. If American shows are shown in country, watch them with host country people and notice their reactions. Ask them why they like these shows.

4. Notice who watches which shows. Does the family watch any shows together? Which do they never watch together? Who decides what to watch?

VI. MOVIES & THEATER PRODUCTION

1. Go to any locally or regionally made movies or theater production and notice the stories and themes. Notice audience reactions. Which scenes do they enjoy the most? Which scenes get the biggest reactions from them? What qualities do the heroes or the villains have? Who makes up the audience?

2. Go to American or other foreign-made films and notice audience reactions. Ask people why they come to these films. Ask them which films they like better: American/western-made or locally made. Why?

VII. SONGS & MUSIC

1. Listen to local or regionally produced songs with an informant and ask him or her to tell you what the lyrics are about. What kind of music and songs are the most popular?

2. Listen to American or foreign music with your informant and ask what he or she thinks of it. Who are the most popular local and foreign singers? Why? Is American music popular? Which artists?

5—CRITICAL INCIDENTS ✎

Another way to learn about culture is through your own critical incidents, moments you remember because of their emotional intensity. You may have gotten furious at the post office, for example, because people kept cutting in line, or maybe you were shouted at on the bus for something you still don't understand. On their own, these incidents don't necessarily teach you anything about the country or culture, but if you reflect on and analyze them, you almost always learn something from them. Here is a four-step method for deconstructing a critical incident.

1. Recollect the incident after you have calmed down, but not so long afterwards that you forget the details.

2. Write down all you can remember about it: what you did and said; what others did and said.

3. Get more information. The easiest way is to relate the incident to anyone you think can help you understand it better, including, if possible, anyone else who was involved in it. Another way is to revisit the scene where the incident occurred, in an observer role, and see if you can find clues to explain what happened.

4. Review the incident from the perspective of this new knowledge and see if you now understand it. You may not understand it completely, but you may understand it better or understand parts of it. And record this entire process in your journal.

6—STUDYING AN INSTITUTION* ✍

An excellent way to learn about a culture is to study a specific institution, whether a private, commercial, educational, charitable, or government enterprise. A sample of institutions in different fields are listed below; you may be able to identify still others in your community:

Agriculture—an animal farm; produce farm; banana, cocoa, or coffee plantation; ag extension office; a retailer or wholesaler of agricultural supplies; distributor of meat or produce.

Arts—a theater company; community theater; an art gallery; a museum of art; an orchestra or some other professional music ensemble; art or textile coop.

Communications—a radio or TV station; newspaper plant; magazine publisher; movie theater.

Educational—a day-care center; nursery; kindergarten; primary school; middle school; high school; vocational school; private academy.

Government—an agency or department; a court; the office of a legislator or government official; any part of the military; any public works department or branch.

Health and Welfare—a hospital; clinic; home for the aged; drug rehabilitation center; physician's office; health education center; an AIDS clinic.

Manufacturing—an assembly plant; a manufacturing plant or factory; food or mineral processing plant.

Public Services—a library; recreational center; police station; public park.

Religion—a church; mosque; temple; monastery; convent; seminary; church run orphanage, coop, or recreation center or school.

Retailing—a department store, pharmacy; bookstore; newsstand; grocery store; restaurant; cafe; corner store; shoestore; office supply store; furniture store; etc.

It's best to choose an institution with which someone you know is connected. You need the institution's cooperation for a study that may take several weeks. Once you begin, try to be as systematic as possible, recording your results in a notebook set up for this purpose. Expect to do both interviewing and observing. The topics and sample questions on the next page may help get you started.

Purpose— Why was the institution begun? What purposes does it serve?

Ownership— Who owns the institution? How did they get to be owners? Why do they want to own such an institution? What impact does their ownership have on the product or service?

Clients— Who are the clients? How does the institution get clients? Does it have enough, too many, too few?

Management— Who runs the institution? How did this person get this position? How is the institution organized for management purposes? Who reports to whom (request or draw an organizational chart)?

Capital Resources— How much money does the institution have? What are its annual expenses? What reserves, debts does it have? What is its annual revenue, profit or loss?

Raw Materials— What raw materials does it need? Where does it get them? How does it get them to the facility, store, or plant? What do they cost? What does transportation cost? Does it keep a large inventory? Where? How does the institution select its suppliers?

Building/ Plant Office— Where is the institution housed? How much does this place cost to lease, or what did it cost to buy? Who maintains it? What does it cost for upkeep, for insurance? How was the location chosen?

Equipment— What equipment does the institution have? How was it obtained? How much did it cost? How is it kept in working order? How much does it cost to maintain?

Supplies— What supplies does the institution need to operate? What do these cost? What's the source? Do other suppliers exist? How is the decision made as to whom to buy from?

Workers— How many people work here? What qualifications do they need? How big is the payroll (weekly, monthly)? How did most of these people get their jobs? What benefits do they get? What do these benefits cost the institution per employee?

Procedures— How do people learn what they have to do? Are procedures many or few? Who sets the procedures?

Distributors— How does the institution handle distribution? What are the costs? How does it select a distributor?

Licenses & Permits— Does this institution need official approval to operate? How is it obtained? How much do these permits, etc. cost? How often do they have to be renewed? Who decides whether an institution gets one and on what basis is this decision made?

Competitors— Who are the competitors? What does the institution do to stay competitive or be ahead of the competition?

* J. Daniel Hess. The Whole World Guide to Cultural Learning, reprinted with permission of Intercultural Press, Inc., Yarmouth, ME. Copyright, 1994.

ANSWERS ✐

CHAPTER ONE

1.3—What is Culture? The Iceberg: Suggested answers

The following items are in the visible part of the iceberg:

1, 3, 5, 7, 10, 11, 15, 16, 21, and 22.

These items are in the invisible part:

2, 4, 6, 8, 9, 12, 13, 14, 17, 18, 19, 20, 23, 24, and 25.

1.5—Linking Values to Behaviors: Suggested answers

1. Directness—Disagreeing openly with someone at a meeting
2. Centrality of family—Taking off from work to attend the funeral of an aunt
3. External Control—Accepting, without question, that something can't be changed
4. Saving face—At a meeting, agreeing with a suggestion you think is wrong
5. Respect for age—Not laying off an older worker whose performance is weak
6. Informality—Asking people to call you by your first name
7. Deference to authority—Asking the headmaster's opinion about something you're the expert on
8. Indirectness—Use of understatement
9. Self-reliance—Not helping the person next to you on an exam
10. Egalitarianism—Inviting the teaboy to eat lunch with you in your office

1.6—Universal/Cultural/Personal: Suggested Answers

Universal behaviors: 2, 8, 12, 13

Cultural behaviors: 3, 4, 5, 9, 10, 11, 14

Personal behaviors: 1, 6, 7, 15

1.10—Defining Culture: List of characteristics of culture

1. culture is collective, shared by a group
2. culture is learned
3. it has to do with values, beliefs, assumptions, attitudes, and feelings
4. it involves customs and traditions
5. it influences or guides behavior

6. it is transmitted from generation to generation

7. it is unconscious or implicit

8. it is a response/adaptation to reality

FUNDAMENTALS OF CULTURE I

I.1—Sharing the Rewards: Answer and Discussion

Person A: $5000

Person B: $5000

Person C: $5000

Person D: $5000

People in collectivist cultures seek the good of the group over the good of themselves, not because they are indifferent to their own welfare, but because they feel the surest way to guarantee personal survival is to make sure the group thrives and prospers. Hence, it would be more important and comforting to me for everyone in my group to benefit as much as possible from this bonus, getting the maximum each person could get ($5000), than for me personally to get more because I happened to do more work. If the person who was only able to do 10% of the work (not that we would even bother to make these calculations, mind you) only got $2000, I would worry about that person's financial well being. If that person suffers from financial need, then his/her performance at work might slip, and then we would *all* be in trouble.

I.2—The Concept of Self: Suggested Answers

These behaviors are *more* commonly associated with individualism:

2—a cocktail party means, generally, superficial contact with a lot of people; collectivists associate intensely with a few people

4—singles out an individual

6—rewards based on what you do, not who you are (which is more collectivist)

7—contracts keep people honest; collectivists know people will be honest (or they get booted out of the group)

8—individuals need their independence

9—because there is no loyalty to the organization (the collective)

10—collectivists shun conflict because it could damage harmony

12—long-term relationships tie the individual down; also individualists move a lot, are less loyal to place

13—collectivists prefer self-effacement

15—fostering independence and taking responsibility for self

16—instead of "other-help" books

20—collectivists would provide for everyone, and then expect to be provided for in turn later on

These behaviors are more commonly associated with collectivism:

1—giving *your* name would be more individualist

3—within a group, collectivists stick together; *vis a vis* other groups, they can be very competitive

5—in the sense that older, senior people are listened to, and they tend to be more traditional

11—people are defined by what they belong to

14—saving face maintains harmony, the glue that keeps the group together

17—so no one feels left out (as opposed to majority rules, which leaves the minority out)

18—the need to be more specific about relationships is more important to collectivists

19—these keep the group, your family, happy (which in turn keeps you happy)

I.3—Score Yourself: Individualism or Collectivism: Results

The following choices tend to be more characteristic of <u>individualists</u>:

1b, 2b, 3a, 4a, 5b, 6b, 7b, 8a, 9a, 10b

These choices tend to be more characteristic of <u>collectivists</u>:

1a, 2a, 3b, 4b, 5a, 6a, 7a, 8b, 9b, 10a

CHAPTER TWO

2.2—The Things We Say: Suggested Answers

1-3: Americans value action and doing over talking, especially if it's talking *instead of* action.

4-6: Directness.

7-8: Emphasis on accomplishment, achieving things, in addition to being a good person.

9-11: Optimism.

12: Self-determination, control over one's destiny

13: Self-reliance, independence.

14-15: Don't judge or be fooled by appearances; look beneath the surface.

16: Risk taking, experimentation.

2.4—Thinking About My Job: Brief notes

For each incident, here are some things you might have thought about or considered.

1. *Attitude Towards Age*—You will need to establish your credibilty with some results that can't be refuted. Or you can ally yourself with someone in the village who does have credibility and who can vouch

for you. You should also be patient; give people time to feel comfortable with you and to see that you aren't leaving tomorrow or next week.

2. *Attitude Towards Change*—Faster and efficient doesn't mean much if these teachers have to learn a whole new way of doing something, especially if they aren't even good at it. Your best chance is probably to give some kind of demonstration and let the technique itself, not your characterization of it, win them over. Or sell someone the teachers look up to on the merits of the technique.

3. *Concept of Equality*—Unless you can enlist other backers for your plan, you should probably drop it. Do you even know if the teaboy would want to be inside? After all, he has survived like this for many years, after all.

4. *Attitude Towards Taking Risks*—Can you try this on a small scale first, so there isn't so much at stake? Is it worth risking your relationship with this man just for the sake of your experiment? Think this through, for your sake and the village's.

5. *View of the Natural World*—The students are obviously used to being taught without books (for a few weeks, anyway). Can't you somehow manage? Will anyone back you in your scheme? What would the price of victory be?

2.5—Sources of American Culture: Suggested Answers

A. Protestantism: 7, 11, 13, 18

B. American Geography: 1, 3, 4, 9, 14, 19, 21

C. Escape from Repression: 2, 5, 6, 10, 12, 15, 16, 22, 23

D. Nature of the Immigrant: 8, 17, 20, 24

Note: Nos. 2, 9, and 18 might also go under D.

2.6—How Non-Americans See Americans: Results

Qualities <u>most</u> associated, in rank order:

    1. Energetic

    2. Industrious

    3. Inventive

    4. Friendly

Qualities <u>least</u> associated, in rank order:

    1. Lazy

    2. Sexy

    3. Honest

    4. Sophisticated

2.8—Now What? Brief notes

1. *Come With Us*—Ask him how important his religion is to him. When he says "very," tell him you feel the same way about yours. Maybe ask him if he would come to your church if he were in your country. Keep

making excuses; the issue might go away. Or compromise and say you aren't able to go to a service but you would like to hear more about his religion.

2. *Aren't You Normal?*—This is very personal, but you will have to weigh the costs of coming out in such a place against those of not coming out. Your best move here is to find another gay PCV and ask him how he has dealt with this. You need advice. Meanwhile, if you want to buy time, you can try to ignore the question.

3. *Native Speaker*—You can try explaining that Americans have very different backgrounds. You may be able to have some other credible native speaker vouch for you. Are there host country native speakers whose families came from elsewhere that you can compare yourself to?

4. *Help*—As a blind person, you have probably encountered this syndrome even in the U.S. Try doing what you have done before. You might also try to explain the cultural difference here, that in the U.S. blind people are often fully functioning members of society and you, as a result, don't know how to handle all the "wonderful" help you are being offered. You can also try saying that you don't want to be a burden on people.

5. *Doubt*—You may have to inform these students in the ways of America. Is there a minority group in the host country that you could compare Blacks in America to, a group that achieves as well as the majority culture?

6. *Manual Labor*—Can you work through an intermediary? You stay on the ground giving explicit instructions while he climbs up and demonstrates? Can you stand nearby so that the workers can easily come to you for instruction?

2.9—Diversity Lessons: Suggested List

1. You are not as relaxed.

2. You listen more and talk less.

3. You may outwardly agree with things you would normally not agree with, because you are the only one who seems to think differently.

4. You refrain from telling certain of your standard stories.

5. In general, you monitor what you say very closely.

6. You are much more alert to feedback, to how people are reacting to you.

7. You observe more closely than you normally do.

8. You don't assume most people agree with you.

9. You don't assume most people understand you.

10. You assume you are being watched and listened to more closely than normal.

11. You don't trust your instincts as much as you normally do.

Fundamentals of Culture II

II.1—An Accident: Discussion

There could be many explanations for the gap here, but one of them almost certainly is the difference between being a universalist (many Americans) and a particularist (many Venezuelans). Universalists tend to feel that right is right, regardless of circumstances, while particularists tend to feel you always have to take circumstances (the person in trouble here is your friend) into account. This section of the workbook will explore these differences in greater detail.

II.2—Personal and Societal Obligations: Suggested Answers

In the first set, #3. is particularist; the other three are universalist because:

1—particularists would say personal feelings would have to be taken into account

2—deals change when circumstances change for particularists

4—for particularists, the law depends on who you are, etc.

In the second set, #1 is universalist; the other three are particularist because:

2—this is particularist dogma

3—particularists are subjective; universalists are objective

4—universalist logic is of the head

In the third set, #1 is particularist; the other three are universalist because:

2—particularists avoid consistency because things are relative

3—particularist logic is of the heart

4—particularists live by exceptions; there are no absolutes

In the fourth set, #2 is universalist; the other three are particularist because:

1—because friends can always be trusted (and you don't do business with strangers anyway)

3—particularist logic says the bond is more important than the facts of the case

4—collectivists have the same in-group/out-group mentality as particularists do

In the fifth set, #4 is universalist; the other three are particularist because:

1—this is particularist dogma, no absolutes

2—particularists always take circumstances into account

3—relationships, the personal side of things, are more important than cost, etc.

II.3—Score Yourself: Universalism or Particularism: Results

The following behaviors tend to be more characteristic of <u>universalists</u>:

1a, 2a, 3b, 4b, 5a, 6a, 7a, 8b, 9b, 10b

These behaviors tend to be more characteristic of <u>particularists</u>:

1b, 2b, 3a, 4a, 5b, 6b, 7b, 8a, 9a, 10a

CHAPTER THREE

3.2-Styles of Communication: Indirect and Direct: Suggested Answers

The following behaviors are commonly associated with high context cultures:

1—high context people have that kind of instinctive understanding common with twins

2—a refusal threatens harmony, which is key in high context cultures

3—what's in the lines is whatever saves face, so the message is between the lines

4—third party communication avoids direct confrontation

5—understatement is more indirect

9—where it's difficult to say no, yes has less meaning

12—relationships are more important in high context cultures, and small talk cements relationships

14—the message is often not in the words in high context cultures, so look for it in something else

17—close-knit networks are common in more collectivist, high context cultures

18—the message is not in the words, so it may be in something else

20—so you won't be upset

The following behaviors are commonly associated with low context cultures:

6—directness is preferred

7—to disagree is common in low context cultures, where one speaks one's mind, no matter whom one is speaking to

8—words are taken more literally

10—acquaintances have to spell things out because they do not instinctively understand each other

11—because the meaning is in the words

13—the task is more important in low context cultures

15—there is rarely any message in the context in low context cultures

16—because networks are less common

19—the words will carry the meaning, not the context: Possible perceptions

3.4—Culture and Communication Styles: Possible perceptions

1. Direct: Americans (on the left side of the continuum) are sometimes seen as blunt and insensitive by HCNs on the left.

2. Low Context: Americans (left side) just don't pick up on any of our cues. You have to spell everything out for them.

3. Face Less Important: Americans (left side) tend to say whatever comes into their head, no matter the situation nor to whom they are talking.

4. The Task: Americans (left side) think you can separate the doer from the deed. You can't get anything done by focusing exclusively on the what; you also have to focus on the who and the how.

3.6—Dialogues: Analysis

In reading these analyses, assume for the sake of the exercise that culture was in fact at the heart of the misunderstanding. These kinds of misunderstandings *can* occur between people from the same culture, of course, but *every* misunderstanding that occurs between people from two different cultures is not caused by a cultural difference, but it is always a *possible* cause and should never be dismissed.

1. Quick Trip

Reading between the lines here, it appears the co-op was "interviewing" the PCV for some kind of expertise he might be able to provide. It sounds like the customary procedure at the co-op is to give people a tour that goes on for at least two hours. If this is a high context culture, then this departure from the norm (a norm the PCV would be expected to know) *may* be a way of sending a signal, which is why the HCN has picked up on this point. The HCN's suspicions only increase when she hears that the people at the co-op scheduled the visit of another expert on the heels of the PCV *and volunteered this information to the PCV*. Again, this *could* mean the people at the co-op want the PCV to know that other candidates are being considered, which in turn *could be* their way of politely indicating he does not have the assignment.

2. Committee Meeting

The mistake here is assuming that if people have a problem with a proposal at a meeting, they'll tell you, even in front of other people. While this may be characteristic behavior in direct, low context cultures, it is less common in indirect cultures. Indirect communicators, worried about face saving and wanting to preserve harmony, usually try to avoid public confrontation. They will avoid discussing a matter rather than clash over it in public (which may be why there was no discussion here) and even say "fine" when things aren't fine. The PCV makes the mistake of assuming that no comment means approval, as it often does in the United States, and that a person who says "fine" is pleased. But the worse error here (worse than these misinterpretations) may be bringing up a potentially controversial topic in a public forum like this, especially if this is the first time the subject has been raised.

3. We'll Get Back To You

Remember that in high context cultures the message is often not found in what people say or do but in what they fail to say or do. In this dialogue, it may be significant that the director did not meet with the PCV as originally planned but instead sent his assistant. And it may be of further significance that the assistant asked few questions and scheduled no subsequent appointment. In other words, no one is going to specifically tell the PCV that there is no interest in her proposal—that could cause an embarrassing loss of face—but the message is nevertheless going to be communicated.

The other possibility, of course, is that there is a perfectly innocent explanation for all this: the director was unavoidably detained at the last minute; the assistant had few questions because she knew the proposal very well; and no new meeting date was set because the assistant simply forgot! The point is that in some cases in some cultures, you may need to read more into the nonverbal communication.

4. Explanations

Miss Chung is trying to save the PCV's face here. After all, if Miss Chung says she doesn't understand the explanation, then the PCV might feel badly that he didn't give a very clear explanation, which the PCV might find embarrassing. Moreover, Miss Chung expects that the PCV will understand that her "yes" may only be for politeness sake. At least this is how it would work in Miss Chung's culture, where one has to be careful not to embarrass an expert. But in more direct cultures, "yes" has a tendency to means yes (not "I'm being polite"), and no one is upset if another person doesn't understand the explanation. Typically, there is less face for the losing and saving in direct cultures than in indirect ones.

5. Transfer

There's a good chance the PCV has misread this exchange and is not being transferred. On the surface—which one learns to be wary of in indirect/high context cultures—the director has been sympathetic and understanding, but she does not appear at any point to have specifically said she will transfer the PCV. That in itself is meaningful. All she *has* said is that she knows Radu is a boor and that she's had a lot of complaints about him. If the PCV sees a transfer in those words, that's his prerogative, but remember that in indirect cultures people often go to great lengths to avoid using the word no, to avoid a scene, and will happily say yes whenever the opportunity presents itself—and even, on occasion, when it doesn't.

3.8—Practicing Indirectness: Suggestions

1. *Do you think that's a good idea?*

    Are there any other ideas?

    I like most parts of that idea.

2. *That's an interesting point.*

    That's another good point.

3. *I have one possible suggestion.*
>> *What do you think of this idea?*

4. *Does anyone else have any suggestions?*
>> *Have we heard all the opinions?*

5. *I have some other figures here.*
>> *Those figures may be slightly old.*

6. *I would do that like this.*
>> *Have you tried doing that this way?*

7. *I have another idea.*
>> *What do you think of this idea?*
>> *May I make a suggestion?*

3.9—Decoding Indirectness: Suggestions

1. *That is a very interesting viewpoint.*
>> *I don't agree.*
>> *We need to talk more about this.*
>> *You're wrong.*

2. *This proposal deserves further consideration.*
>> *We don't like it.*
>> *It needs work.*
>> *Propose something else.*

3. *I know very little about this, but....*
>> *I'm something of an expert on this but am too polite to say so.*
>> *What I think we should do is...*

4. *We understand your proposal very well.*
>> *Do you have another one?*
>> *We don't like it.*

5. *We will try our best.*
>> *Don't expect much to happen.*

6. *I heard another story about that project.*
>> *I don't agree with what you said about that project.*

7. *Can we move on to the next topic?*
>> *We don't want to talk about this now.*
>> *We need to consult with people not in the room before we can decide.*

3.10—Harmony and Face: Brief notes

1. *Crop Failure*—Heap praise upon his scheme and then delicately point out how one or two tiny parts of it (the core) might not work. Or let

him know your opinion through an intermediary so he doesn't get embarrassed in front of you.

2. *End Run*—Is the pace of your project truly unbearable? Is it going nowhere or going somewhere with exquisite (and excruciating) slowness? Would patience help? What about explaining the situation to an HCN colleague and getting advice? Are you sure you know how the division manager would react if you went around the supervisor?

3. *Moving Up*—How much does it matter? Will things go to hell in a handbasket if this person is promoted? Can you plead ignorance? Will it cost you anything to be honest?

4. *Electronic Mail*—Don't forget that your boss may also know the facts here. Mention how good the company it is in *other* ways, and then ask whether your boss knows if this company has any experience in this area. Talk around the point, without leaving any doubt where you stand (or any fingerprints on the gun).

5. *Tight Spot*—This is messy. Pleading ignorance is probably a good bet here.

FUNDAMENTALS OF CULTURE III

III.1—Service With a Smile: Drawing

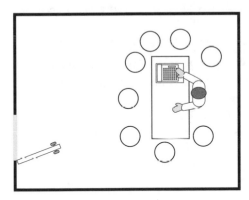

III.2—The Concept of Time: Monochronic & Polychronic: Suggested Answers

These behaviors are more commonly associated with the monochronic world view:

1—time is just time for polychronic types

2—being on time is important for monochronic types

3—monochronic time depends on schedules

4—monochronic time thinks less about people, more about goals

7—changes in plans upset monochronic people who live by their plans

8—because it takes other people into account less than polychronic time

15—because being late is rude in monochronic time

17—because they upset the schedule

18—being waited on one at a time is monochronic behavior

These behaviors are more commonly associated with the polychronic world view:

5—waiting isn't bad in cultures where being on time is less important

6—upsetting schedules doesn't matter where schedules aren't that important anyway

9—people count more in polychronic time

10—in that collectivists are more attuned to needs of others, as are polychronic types

11—being on time (adhering to deadline) not as crucial in polychronic world

12—late matters less where time matters less

13—polychronic types are more in touch with the person than monochronic types

14—polychronic types can change plans more easily because they are less in the grip of schedules

16—there is always enough time in polychronic world

III.3—Score Yourself: Monochronic and Polychronic: Results

The following behaviors tend to be more characteristic of <u>monochronic</u> people:

1a, 2b, 3a, 4b, 5a, 6a, 7b, 8a, 9b, 10b

The following behaviors tend to be more characteristic of <u>polychronic</u> people:

1b, 2a, 3b, 4a, 5b, 6b, 7a, 8b, 9a, 10a

CHAPTER FOUR

4.2-The Concept of Power: Suggested Answers

These behaviors are more commonly associated with high power distance cultures:

1—there is more fear of displeasing the boss in high power distance cultures

2—emphasizing distinctions between boss and subordinates is the norm

5—rank has its privileges in these cultures

7—again, to emphasize the distance

8—close supervision, the visible exercise of power, is common to these cultures

11—the unequal distribution of power

12—independence is not valued in subordinates

14—to keep those with and without power separated

15—rank must be respected; you should not go around people

16—there is a need to show who has power over whom

17—bosses are supposed to wield their power

19—to emphasize the power gap

These behaviors are more commonly associated with low power distance cultures:

3—because superiors do not have to be deferred to

4—no one is threatened by independence or thinking for oneself

6—power differences are not emphasized

9—because the distance is minimized

10—we're all equal here so we all depend on each other

13—because he's just another worker here

18—because we are all in this together, power distance is de-emphasized

4.4—Dialogues: Analysis

In reading these analyses, assume for the sake of the exercise that culture was in fact at the heart of the misunderstanding. These kinds of misunderstandings *can* occur between people from the same culture, of course, but *every* misunderstanding that occurs between people from two different cultures is not caused by a cultural difference, but it is always a *possible* cause and should never be dismissed out of hand.

1. Bosses Have Their Reasons

In many high power distance cultures, bosses are not used to having their decisions questioned or, worse, having to explain them to subordinates. In such cultures, bosses make decisions, and subordinates carry them out. And if there *are* questions, they would normally be raised in a most delicate manner and always through the proper channels. The HCN has been trying to suggest all this to the PCV ("She must have her reasons." "She's the boss."), but the Volunteer hasn't been listening. This doesn't mean bosses are unapproachable or infallible, but you do have to think long and hard before challenging those in power, and to then do so in the appropriate way.

2. A Surprise for the Chief

Chances are Mr. Plonc isn't going to be pleased. In many American workplaces, employees are rewarded and praised for taking the initiative, for seeing something that needs to be done and just doing it, without waiting to be told. In high power distance cultures, that kind of behavior is often interpreted as taking power that hasn't been given to you. You have made a decision that wasn't yours to make, and in the process usurped and threatened the authority of the person who is *supposed* to make such a decision. In cultures where power is highly centralized and closely guarded, taking initiative is a risky business.

3. The Golden Spoon

In high power distance cultures, interaction between the higher ranks and the lower ranks, any mixing of the ranks, is relatively uncommon and tends to be quite formal. Provincial representatives don't just have lunch with the little guys on the spur of the moment; most people would feel quite uncomfortable and awkward. In these cultures, people of higher status tend not to regard themselves as being like workers, nor do they want to be seen that way. The greater the gulf between the higher ranks and the lower echelons, the better for everyone. A casual lunch invitation, as suggested by the PCV in this dialogue, would not be the norm, and if the representative accepted, the supervisors he would normally lunch with might take it as a deliberate slight.

4. A Lesson

The person learning the lesson here may turn out to be the PCV, not Mr. Biswas. The PCV is apparently planning to take an important matter directly to the dean, without informing Mr. Biswas. In many cultures, this bypassing of the chain of command will not be appreciated. Indeed, the first question from the dean to the PCV is likely to be: "Did you discuss this with Mr. Biswas?"

Even if Mr. Biswas is as ineffective as everyone claims, that doesn't mean it's acceptable to go around him. The proper thing would be for the PCV to engage Biswas on the matter, see if he responds, and if he doesn't, then either announce that he's going to the dean or ask Biswas to do so. If Biswas still does nothing, then the PCV can go to the dean with relative impunity, having gone through the proper channels.

4.5-Attitude Toward Uncertainty: Suggested Answers

These behaviors are more commonly associated with high uncertainty avoidance cultures:

1—because sticking to the structure, the schedule, is comforting

2—when people lose control of emotions, anything can happen!

3—because it is unpredictable or unknown

5—being formal assures a certain order in the unfolding of interactions

9—going around the structure threatens it's very survival, and where would we be without structure?

11—these cultures are comforted by expertise, and that is gained by long study; the common person couldn't know that much

12—conflict threatens the smooth running of things

14—stability is sought and provided for; change is threatening

15—because of the fear of the unknown

17—authority guarantees order and keeps things under control

19—rules are the foundation of order

21—risks are inherently unsettling because they involve the unknown

These behaviors are more commonly associated with low uncertainty avoidance cultures:

4—change is not so frightening

6—differing views are nothing to be afraid of; nothing is set in stone

7—you can't know or control the future anyway

8—there's nothing to fear from emotions

10—order doesn't break down or get undermined that easily

13—the unknown is not frightening

16—there isn't that much fear and what can't be understood or controlled

18—control is not that comforting

20—rules can be limiting; there's nothing inherently satisfying about rules

22—since the unknown isn't particularly worrying, risks are not to be feared

4.6—Dialogues: Analysis

In reading these analyses, assume for the sake of the exercise that culture was in fact at the heart of the misunderstanding. These kinds of misunderstandings *can* occur between people from the same culture, of course, nor is *every* misunderstanding that occurs between people from two different cultures caused by a cultural difference, but it is always a *possible* cause and should never be dismissed out of hand.

1. About Manuel

On the whole, people in high uncertainty avoidance cultures try to steer clear of confrontation and conflict. They believe that conflict is potentially destabilizing, that unless people keep their feelings in check, things can get dangerously out of hand. Thus, Manuel will probably not confront his boss, though at some later point, when he has calmed down, they may have a civilized conversation about the matter. The PCV's notion that getting things off your chest is better than seething may not fit this culture.

2. In Over His Head

People in high uncertainty avoidance cultures like certainties, and in this regard nothing comforts quite so much as an expert. One can rely on experts, comforted by their command of their field; they can tell you what's going to happen and what to do about it. Or, if they can't quite do that, they can at least help you devise strategies and responses to handle whatever might happen. In this kind of world, experts do not like to admit mistakes and let down those who depend on them (nor do those people like to be disappointed in this regard). So the expert from the capital, whatever else he may do, is not going to admit he made a mistake. He will probably announce one day that we are going to try something new—and that will be that.

3. Regulations

Laws, policies, regulations and procedures are a great comfort to people who are frightened by uncertainty, for the simple reason that they prescribe—or at least attempt to prescribe—human behavior. If you have laws, you don't have to worry about how people are going to behave; you *know* how they're going to behave. And that makes life infinitely more certain and predictable. In such societies, ignoring or circumventing the law is a serious matter. If a law makes no sense, as it sometimes does in unusual circumstances, then make a new one to fit those circumstances. But whatever you do, don't break the original law.

4. Backlog

Another characteristic of uncertainty avoiding cultures is fear of the new and of change. What's new or different is inherently risky, and risk is uncertainty personified. Note the hesitation of the HCN in this dialogue, trying to find out if this new software has ever been tried in "organizations like ours." If it has, then the risk is less and therefore more palatable. But it has only been tried in America, which isn't much comfort. Another problem, of course, is that everyone will have to be trained in the software, a further complication in a culture which likes the status quo. All together, it would be better to wait until next summer and resubmit the request. Getting rid of the backlog just isn't worth the risk of all this experimentation.

4.8—The Source of Status: Brief notes

1. *Upstanding Students*—Is this behavior really worth resisting? Pick your battles carefully when you are a PCV.

2. *Respect*—This does not seem a stand worth taking. Weigh how much it will cost you to continue confusing workers (who are not from an egalitarian culture like yours) against whatever personal satisfaction you may derive from just being yourself.

3. *In the Matter of Mr. Kodo*—With luck you can sidestep this issue and say that as an outsider you do not want to get involved. Or you can say that you are sympathetic to Mr. Kodo but do not feel that a public campaign is the right way to resolve such issues. If you would like to go further and declare your position on the matter, in favor of the choice that was made, then you might couch it in cultural terms and say that Americans take more than loyalty and longevity into account in making such decisions. Whatever you do, there is nothing to be lost for expressing your sympathy for Mr. Kodo.

4. *Considering the Source*—Depending on the country here, you may be stuck. If your boss is not into raising awareness, and he's right about the attitudes of the delegation, you risk achieving the ends you want (policy changes) by objecting to the means.

4.9—Workplace Values and Norms: Possible perceptions

The mark indicating the American position is normally on the left side on all of these continuums.

1. Power distance: HCNs might think Americans don't respect bosses very much. Or that bosses are entirely too chummy with subordinates.

2. Uncertainty avoidance: Americans take too many risks and don't respect traditions enough.

3. Source of status: Achievements matter too much to Americans. They don't believe in the wisdom of experience or the significance of one's social class and upbringing.

4. Concept of work: Americans can't enjoy life because work and success matter too much to them.

5. Personal/professional: Americans try to separate life into artificial boxes. It's not as black and white as they think. Life is gray.

6. Motivation: Americans think too much about the professional side of work and life; they should worry more about the human side. They want to get ahead, but for what? We all die, even those who are ahead.

7. Key to productivity: Americans are too fixated on output and results, the what; they aren't concerned enough about the how. They don't realize the how affects the what.

8. Ideal worker: Anybody can have skills (or get them); what matters is personal qualities. Americans focus on the superficial, what the person can do; they should focus on the substance, on who the person is.

4.11—You Americans: Notes

These are some suggestions as to why Americans come across the way they do to HCNs:

1. Why are you Americans always in such a hurry to get things done?

   We often seem this way because of our tendency to use achievements and accomplishments as a measure of a person's worth. We're in a hurry to get things done because it's only then that we feel we have proved our worth.

2. Why do you Americans insist on treating everyone the same?

   We do this because of a deep cultural instinct toward egalitarianism, which was a reaction to the class system and, before that, the feudal system that existed in Europe. In cultures where inequality is more accepted, our insistence on egalitarianism may be grating.

3. Why do you Americans always have to say what you're thinking?

> We believe that being direct is the most efficient way to communicate. And being more efficient means you get more done.

4. Why do you Americans always want to change things?

> We think things can always be better, that progress is inevitable. Older cultures are more skeptical because they have been around longer and seen more.

5. Why don't you Americans show more respect for your seniors and elders?

> We respect results, not age or authority. Therefore, unless an elder or a senior also happens to be a superior achiever, there is no automatic respect.

6. Why do you Americans always think things are going to get better?

> We are optimists because we believe the locus of control is in ourselves. Therefore, the only obstacle to things getting better is a personal lack of will or effort, which is eminently fixable.

7. Why are you Americans so concerned about individual recognition?

> Individualism is ingrained in us. Not being used to working together that much, we don't trust team or group recognition.

8. Why are you Americans so impatient?

> If things take a long time to do, we can do fewer of them. And when you're counting achievements, more is better.

4.13—Turning the Tables

1. Keep working at the language. Your efforts alone will impress people, and the advances you make will impress them even more.

2. Try your hand at some small task you *know* you will succeed at. This will establish your basic competence and improve your standing.

3. Do _not_ take on anything ambitious or high profile, until you are very sure of yourself. An early failure can leave a lasting impression.

4. Listen. Listen. And then listen further. If you listen to people, they'll know you know something—because they told you.

5. Spend time with colleagues and coworkers, on and off the job. As people see you interacting with others—and with them—they'll assume you are learning things about their culture, etc. On the other hand, if you hang around with the other PCV in town and go away on the weekends, they'll assume you're not learning very much.

6. Ask questions, all the time, of everyone. People will be impressed that you are asking. And besides, you need to learn as much as you can, and then let people know you have learned.

7. Work with someone who *is* credible. People may not entrust you with responsibilities on your own, but they may entrust you and your host country partner with important work.

8. Try to exhibit as much cultural sensitivity as possible. Nothing hurts your credibility quite so much as stories about the faux pas you have made. And nothing helps it as much as stories about your sensitivity.

9. Be patient. The sheer passing of time will work to your advantage; people will get used to your being around and see you less and less as an outsider.

FUNDAMENTALS OF CULTURE IV

IV.1—Who's In Charge Here? Discussion

There could be many explanations, but one almost certainly is the fact that many Americans believe in the power of the individual to prevail against all obstacles, that there is nothing people cannot do or become if they want it badly enough and are willing to make the effort. This notion is best exemplified in the classic American expression: "Where there is a will there is a way."

In Chinese culture, many people believe that while you can shape your life to some extent, certain external forces, things beyond your control, also play an important part. What happens to you in life is not entirely in your hands.

IV.2—The Locus of Control: Suggested answers

In the first set, #1 is external; the others are internal because:

2—this is core of internal dogma

3—as people figure out more and more about the world

4—if the world is a mechanism, then it's possible to know how it works; no problem should be unsolvable if you look hard enough

In the second set, #2 is external; the others are internal because:

1—internally controlled people believe humans are in control

3—it's all up to you in the internally controlled world

4—mechanisms (technology) are a hallmark of internally controlled thinking

In the third set, #1 is internal; the others are external because:

2—anything can happen in the external world

3—core of external dogma

4—externally controlled people don't believe man can dominate

In the fourth set, #1 is internal; the others are external because:

2—not everything is knowable

3—you can't necessarily make things happen

4—you can't always be happy because that would mean you were in control

IV.3—Score Yourself: The Locus of Control: Results

The following choices tend to be more characteristic of <u>internally controlled</u> people:

1a, 2a, 3b, 4a, 5b, 6a, 7a, 8b, 9a

The following choices tend to be more characteristic of <u>externally controlled</u> people:

1b, 2b, 3a, 4b, 5a, 6b, 7b, 8a, 9b

CHAPTER FIVE

5.5—What Would You Do? Friendship: Brief Notes

1. *Visa Problems*—There's no harm in trying, and especially not in being seen or known to have tried, even though you know you will get nowhere. (Or do you?) You could also explain that in a universalist culture like yours, the law is the law and connections don't help that much.

2. *Going Away*—Can you plead that because you live alone, it might not be safe? That there isn't always someone around as at the family's home? Can you say you've never done this sort of thing and would fear for the boy's well being? Can you say that without help, such as they always have, you would not be able to pull it off? Can you accept and hire someone to help?

3. *A Parental Visit*—You can try explaining that not introducing one's parents to a friend, especially if there are difficulties involved, doesn't have the same meaning as it does in the host country. You can use the excuses in the story. You can try something else to make up to your friend.

4. *Loan Star*—Try explaining that it isn't so much the money but the whole concept that is the problem. You don't mind doing them a favor, but the real favor would be to get them to examine their premises. You could say the money is needed for some other friend, in worse straits. You could say you can't afford it.

5. *Missing Funds*—Is an audit likely to be done in the next few months? Can you and he arrange a repayment schedule? Can you put the money in and have him repay you? Can he get a loan somewhere else?

5.8—Men and Women: Brief Notes

1. *After Dark*—Be firm and unequivocal. Forget about cultural sensitivity and do what works to get the man out of your house. You might also suggest that he is taking advantage of your ignorance of his culture. You might say that we can talk about this later but that now he simply has to leave. Don't give openings or he might exploit them.

2. *Wedding Bells*—You can say you're not ready for marriage. You can

say your parents would want to approve of any future husband.

3. *Just the Two of Us*—The situation at the school is probably your biggest concern here. As long as you stop the relationship now, at the point you have learned it was not the "innocent" situation you thought it was, you should be able to defend your behavior if anyone maligns you.

4. *A Turning Point*—My, my. Is this really true, that her family would be ruined? Does anyone need to know that you slept together? This sort of thing must happen frequently here. Ask for some advice from HCNs.

5. *Pressure*—No response may be the best response here, except to stop seeing this man. One person calling you a racist, against the considerable evidence that you are not, will not harm you in the end, however painful it may be for you in the meantime. You can also try reasoning with him, of course, and explaining your culture and your personal feelings about a sexual relationship.

6. *Unrequited Feelings*—Chances are this will blow over. Move swiftly to stop the slander.

FUNDAMENTALS OF CULTURE— COMPARING AMERICAN AND HOST COUNTRY VIEWS

1. Self identification: The mark for Americans is normally on the left here. If your host country mark is on the right side, HCNs might perceive Americans as selfish and not caring about others.

2. Egalitarian: The mark here for Americans is normally on the left side. HCNs on the right might think Americans care too much about people in general and not enough about close friends and family, that we are odd for trying to treat everybody like everybody else. Everybody *isn't* like everybody else.

3. Autonomous: Americans, on the left, come across to those on the right as too individualistic, not worrying or caring enough about the greater good, which is what will save us all in the end. Everyone has to work together.

4. Universalism: Americans (on the left) appear to HCNs on the left as too rigid trying to be fair when there is no need to be fair. These HCNs believe you have to take circumstances into account; they make all the difference.

5. Monochronic: Americans (monochronic) are seen by polychronic types as too concerned about time and schedules and not concerned enough about people.

6. One thing at a time: Americans (on the left) are too linear, according to their HCN opposites. They can't enjoy the moment or be spontaneous. They want to be in control.

7. Life is what I do: Americans (on the left) are too driven, too anxious. They don't know how to relax and just let things happen.

8. Progress is inevitable: Americans (on the left) are never satisfied with things as they are. As HCNs on the left see them, Americans always want to make things better.

CHAPTER SIX

6.3—The Cycle of Adjustment: Suggested Answers

1. II (you'll probably get used to them later)
2. IV (when you begin to realize you don't know as much as you think you do)
3. II
4. II
5. I
6. V
7. III
8. I, II, or III but not IV or V
9. III
10. II
11. III or V (depending on the person)
12. V
13. II
14. V (or III for some people)
15. IV
16. IV
17. V
18. I

6.6—The Four Levels of Cultural Awareness: Suggested Answers

1. II or III   *I understand less than I thought I did.*

    II is the better choice here, for by the time you are in III, you begin to understand *more* than you thought you did.

2. I   *These people really aren't so different.*

    Phase I is the only choice here. If you were tempted to put IV, resist: Someone in IV may understand foreigners very well and interact easily with them, but he/she knows quite well that these people are different.

3. III   *There is a logic to how these people behave.*

III is best here, for by now you are not only aware that these people are different (II) but you understand how they are different.

4. II or III   *Living here is like walking on eggshells.*

II is probably the best answer, for it is now beginning to dawn on you how easy it is to make mistakes. Someone in III might feel this way too, but by now you are starting to have more hope of figuring these people out and avoiding mistakes.

5. I   *These people have no trouble understanding me.*

You might have put IV here because you were thinking that a culturally sensitive foreigner would never do anything "foreign" in front of the local people. Someone in IV, however, while finding it easy to understand the local people, would not assume that they would easily understand a foreigner.

6. III   *It's possible to figure these people out if you work at it.*

This is really the only choice here, for someone in II wouldn't necessarily know enough to be able to do this.

7. II or III   *I wonder what they think of me.*

I does not apply here, for people in this phase think they *know* what the local people think of them. IV is out too, because at this level people *do* know what the local people are thinking. In II you would start to wonder, and you could still be wondering in III as well, even as you were getting a grip on the culture.

8. I or IV   *I know what they think of me.*

Those in I believe this mistakenly because they think they are just like the local people, but people in IV *do* know what local people think of them.

9. I or IV   *It's nice to be able to relax and be myself.*

People in I relax because they (wrongly) see nothing to worry about. People in IV can relax and be themselves because they have acquired enough of the local instincts to be able to trust their behavior.

10. II   *I'll never figure these people out.*

This can only be II, for by III you *are* beginning to figure people out.

11. I   *Why did people say this would be so difficult?*

Because it is!

12. III   *There's hope for me here.*

In II you might not be so sure of this, but by III you're starting to see cultural patterns and beginning to have hope.

6.7—Attitudes Toward Cultural Difference—Part Two: Suggested Answers

I. Denial   Paragraph # 6

II. Defense   Paragraph # 7

III. Minimization   Paragraph # 8

IV. Acceptance   First part of paragraph #10

V. & VI. Adaptation & Integration   Last part of paragraph #10

6.10—Can I Still Be Me? Brief notes

1. *Holding Back?*—Can you make your points outside of meetings and still be effective? Can you enlist someone higher up to help you? Can you make your points in the meetings in a way that does not outshine him?

2. *Drawings*—Is there a way to approve the drawings and get them corrected later? Can you approach the division head for a confidential chat? Can you work with the cousin and make sure the drawings arrive at your desk in an approvable form? Can someone else work with this man and correct his drawings? Remember that saving face here is the issue.

3. *Friendly Advice*—Is the charge true? What are the consequences of ignoring the advice? Is this a battle you want to fight at this time? Can you consult other HCNs for their reading of the situation? How strongly do you feel about this?

4. *Good News*—This is a hard one. Will it make any difference if you don't rewrite your report? Will it just be ignored if it isn't favorable? How would you feel about saying no and having someone else rewrite it? Can you tone it down without being dishonest? Maybe you should get some other advice here.

5. *Extrovert*—Get some advice, but if these remarks are representative of the culture, then you may have to adjust your style, unless you are willing to live with the consequences.

6. *Away From Home*—Use explanations these men can accept about why you don't drink or visit prostitutes. You can use a cultural explanation or a personal one, or both. Try to show how your refusals are not personal, and try to spend time with these men in other pursuits, so they see it is not their company that you are avoiding, only these particular events.

This is the Peace Corps' first cross-cultural training workbook designed for independent study. This short evaluation is the first of three evaluations. Part two will survey trainers and part three will survey Volunteers in more detail after they have been in the field for several months (you may be included in this survey). Your feedback will be used to revise the workbook in order to make it more effective. If you have any questions about this evaluation please direct them to Laurette Bennhold-Samaan, Cross-Cultural Specialist, Peace Corps Headquarters or e-mail to lbennhold-samaan@peacecorps.gov. The Training Staff greatly appreciate your input.

After you have completed as much of the workbook as possible, please take a few minutes to complete this evaluation. Please do not place your name or any other identifier on the questionnaire in order to keep your responses anonymous. We know your experience is multifaceted, but please try to answer these questions within the context of the workbook itself. After you have completed the evaluation, place it in an envelope and please return it to your trainer. Thank you for your help on this important project!

YOUR BACKGROUND

1. **Are you:**   1   female   2   male

2. **What is your status?**   1   Trainee   2   Volunteer   3   Trainer   4   Other PC Staff

3. **What country are you serving in?** _____

4. **Date of arrival in country:** ____ ____   **4b. Today's date:** ____ ____ ____
                                  Mo.   Year   Mo.   Day   Year

5. **How much of the workbook have you completed?**

1	2	3	4	5
Not a lot	Less than half	About half	More than half	Entire workbook

6. **Approximately how many hours did it take you to complete this much of the workbook?** _____   *(number of hours)*

7. **How was this workbook used?** *(Circle as many as apply)*

1	2	3	4	5
Self study	w/ other trainees	w/ trainer	In training sessions	Other, specify:

8. **Which method of using the workbook was most effective?** *(Circle only one.)*

1	2	3	4	5
Self study	w/ other trainees	w/ trainer	In training sessions	Other, specify:

WORKBOOK TOPICS & EXERCISES

9. Below is a list of the topics covered in the workbook. Please check if you think that any of the topics need *more exercises* or *fewer exercises*. Also, please check the *5 most important topics*

Topic	Need *More* Exercises	Need *Fewer* Exercises	5 Most Important
a. Culture	❑	❑	❑
b. Concept of Self	❑	❑	❑
c. American Culture	❑	❑	❑
d. Personal v. Societal Obligations	❑	❑	❑
e. Communication Styles	❑	❑	❑
f. Concept of Time	❑	❑	❑
g. Workplace	❑	❑	❑
h. Locus of Control	❑	❑	❑
i. Social Relationships	❑	❑	❑
j. Adjustment Issues	❑	❑	❑
k. Coping Strategies	❑	❑	❑
l. Appendix: Continued Learning	❑	❑	❑
m. Other topics that are not included but that are important: _____	❑	❑	❑
_____	❑	❑	❑

10. **Similar types of exercises were used to cover different topics. Please rate each type of exercise by putting a number in the column which corresponds to the scale. Next to each type of exercise is a page number that provides an <u>example</u>.**

1	2	3	4	5
Ineffective	Not very effective	Effective	Mostly effective	Very effective

Type of Exercise	*Rating*		*Type of Exercise*	*Rating*
a. Score yourself/Rating (p. 34)	____		f. Dear Jan Letter (p. 39)	____
b. Journal (p. 28)	____		g. Continuum (p.81)	____
c. Reflective (p. 73)	____		h. Dialogues (p. 88)	____
d. Observational (p. 84)	____		i. Critical Incidents (p. 171)	____
e. Readings (p. 70)	____			

11. **How important were the Quotes throughout the workbook?**

1	2	3	4	5
Not important	Somewhat important	Important	Mostly important	Very important

12. **How easy was it to find a cultural informant to participate in the workbook activities?**

1	2	3	4	5
Impossible to find	Difficult to find	Varied	Easy to find	Always able to find

WORKBOOK FORMAT AND ORGANIZATION

13. **Please rate the workbook on a scale of 1 to 5 in the following areas:**

1	2	3	4	5
Ineffective	Not very effective	Effective	Mostly effective	Very effective

Area	*Rating*
a. Workbook Organization/Structure	____
b. Workbook Instructions	____

WORKBOOK CONTENT

14. **What was your favorite aspect of the workbook?** _____

_____

15. **What was your least favorite aspect of the workbook?** _____

_____

WORKBOOK EFFECTIVENESS

	Not at all	A little	Somewhat	A lot	Significantly
16. How much has this workbook increased your overall understanding of culture?	1	2	3	4	5
17. How much has this workbook helped you to better understand your experiences in the initial adjustment and training period?	1	2	3	4	5
18. How much has this workbook increased your knowledge of American culture and its influence on your own behavior?	1	2	3	4	5
19. How much has this workbook influenced your communication style with HCNs?	1	2	3	4	5

20. **Do you have any additional comments?** _____

_____

THANK YOU FOR EVALUATING THE WORKBOOK! PLEASE RETURN THIS FORM TO YOUR TRAINER.